MW00354397

VOLCANO: AN A TO Z

Dear Devens —
Thanks so much
for being in our lives

Volcano: an A to Z

and Other Essays about Geology, Geography,

& Geo-Travel in the American West

NEIL MATHISON

BAUHAN PUBLISHING

PETERBOROUGH NEW HAMPSHIRE

2017

© 2017 Neil Mathison
All Rights Reserved

Library of Congress Cataloging-in-Publication Data
Names: Mathison, Neil, author.
Title: Volcano : an A to Z and other essays about geology, geography, and geo-travel in the American West / Neil Mathison.
Other titles: Geology, geography, and geo-travel in the American West
Description: Peterborough, NH : Bauhan Publishing, 2017.
Identifiers: LCCN 2016058530 (print) | LCCN 2017010868 (ebook) | ISBN 9780872332294 (softcover : alk. paper) | ISBN 9780872332300 (ebook)
Subjects: LCSH: Mathison, Neil—Travel—West (U.S.) | Mathison, Neil—Homes and haunts—West (U.S.) | Human being—Effect of environment on—West (U.S.) | Authors, American Biography—21st century | Geology—West (U.S.) | West (U.S.) Geography. | West (U.S.)—Description and travel.
Classification: LCC PS3613.A8288 V65 2017 (print) | LCC PS3613.A8288 (ebook) | DDC 814/.6—dc23
LC record available at https://lccn.loc.gov/2016058530

Book Design by Kirsty Anderson
Cover Design by Henry James
Cover image, *Fine Wind, Clear Morning* from *Thirty-six Views of Mount Fuji* (c. 1830-32) by Katsushika Hokusai (1760-1849)

BAUHAN
PUBLISHINGLLC

PO BOX 117 PETERBOROUGH NEW HAMPSHIRE 03458
603-567-4430
WWW.BAUHANPUBLISHING.COM

Follow us on Facebook and Twitter – @bauhanpub

MANUFACTURED IN THE UNITED STATES OF AMERICA

To Susan

Contents

Acknowledgments

"Maps" appeared in *Cold Mountain Review,* Spring 2013. "Wooden Boat" appeared in *Blue Lyra Review,* Issue 1–2. "My Redwoods" appeared in *Blue Lyra Review* and in *Blue Lyra Review: An Anthology of Diverse Voices,* Vol. 1. "Volcano: an A to Z" appeared in *Southern Humanities Review,* Fall 2008. "Ice" appeared in *North American Review,* Winter 2012. "Catastrophic Columbia" appeared in *Old Growth Northwest,* Spring 2014. "Twenty-two Ways to Lose and (Maybe) Regain Paradise" appeared in *Southern Humanities Review,* Fall 2011.

Maps

MY FATHER, JOHN MATHISON, collected maps, much as a scholar might collect Shakespearean folios or a musicologist Mozart scores. His maps were neither rare nor especially valuable: Rand McNally and AAA road maps—what you have in your car; Coast and Geodetic Survey maps; charts of Puget Sound and the Chesapeake Bay. He marked them with journeys he made and journeys he hoped to make. In 1939, when a young man, he had passionately desired to visit Europe. The beginning of World War II cancelled his first trip. My mother's difficult 1956 pregnancy with my sister Charlotte cancelled a planned second trip. But my father never stopped studying his *Baedekers* and his *National Geographics* and his *Green Guides*, until, finally, in 1960, he took us all to Europe—my mother; my sister, just three; my two brothers, ten and seven; and me, then twelve—driving us in three days from Seattle to New York City so as to catch the cheapest flight, a KLM piston-and-prop DC-7C bound for Shannon, Ireland. I remember landing at the Shannon Airport, pleased to confirm that Ireland was truly green, but surprised to discover that the Irish marked their sheep with dye to distinguish one flock from another and that Irish railway stations smelled like horse manure. On our bus ride from the Shannon Airport to Limerick we passed the ruin of an honest-to-god castle. What would we see next? Knights on horseback? Leprechauns? Banshees? From Limerick we took the trans-Ireland train to Dublin; from Dublin, the overnight steamer to Liverpool; from Liverpool, another train to London's Euston Station. It was the week of Princess Margaret's wedding. The London lampposts were festooned with ribbons and flowers. The Queen's Guards glittered. Londoners greeted us with smiles and laughter, quite unlike the English reserve my parents had told us to expect. But I also remember how my father, having just arrived, guided my brother, Charlie, and me street by street from Euston Square Station to Regents Park, past buildings still bombed out from World War II and red double-decker buses and black London taxicabs and then back again to our modest Euston Square hotel as though he were born a Londoner, the result of his studying his London maps.

The creation of maps preceded writing by thousands of years. The oldest map extant may be celestial, a wall map of the stars Deneb, Altair, and Vega, the Summer Triangle, painted more than seventeen thousand years ago in the Lascaux Caves in southwestern France. I like to picture the map's creators, clad in ice-age furs, drawing by firelight. But I wonder too, were all the tribe members permitted to see it? Or was it a domain exclusive to chiefs and shamans, a Paleolithic equivalent of an exclusive London club?

Maps mirror their zeitgeist. The earth has been described as an oyster, a box, a disk, a column, a ball, and, by Columbus in the last years of his life, as a very round pear. The Babylonians, the Chinese, and the Ancient Greeks all placed themselves at the ethno-center of their maps, while barbarians and unicorns prowled the map edge. As late as the Renaissance, unexplored territories were often marked with the Latin admonitions: "Here be dragons." In medieval times, cartographers drafted T–O maps (also known as O–T maps for the Latin *orbis terrae,* or "circle of the earth"). In T–O maps the world centered on Jerusalem. Europe and Africa occupied the bottom-left and bottom-right quadrants, and Asia the top because the sun rose there, which meant the Garden of Eden had to be in Asia, which meant that Asia was closest to God. T–O maps neglected the southern hemisphere entirely even though most theologians and cartographers of the time agreed the earth was a sphere. But why bother? You couldn't get there. Not through the Torrid Zone; this, as scholars knew, belted the earth's equator with a steamy, impassable barrier. Of course T–O maps weren't intended for travel. T–O maps were intended to show man's place in the cosmos in an age both religious and hierarchical.

* * *

A few years ago, after visiting London several times on business, I took the time to study my own London maps. Piccadilly, Westminster, Charing Cross. The Abbey, St. Paul's, Harrods. Names so familiar, I felt as if I'd known the city my whole life. But I had no idea that the Thames looped through the city like the letter omega. Or why the West End and East End were "ends." Or what Charing

Cross actually crossed. I couldn't understand the connections and by not know-ing London's connections, no matter how well I knew my Sherlock Holmes and my Charles Dickens and my P. D. James, I couldn't begin to know London.

In this I fell short of my father.

My wife Susan also collects maps. Thirty-year-old Michelins that are the mementos of her college-age travels; London Underground maps, Paris Metro maps, Hong Kong and Singapore maps; maps of walking-tours through New York City and sailboat voyages around Vancouver Island. Some of her maps adorn our walls. Some are even valuable. These are the antiques, copper-plate engravings, the originals dating from the seventeenth century. Among their cartographers is a Willem Janszon Blaeu (his name is spelled a variety of ways), a seventeenth-century Dutch mapmaker, who learned his trade under the Danish astronomer Tycho Brahe. Blaeu's maps are printed on heavy, off-white laid paper in black ink, their national and continental boundaries hand-painted in green, yellow, and rose watercolors. The place names are in Latin, the letters so small I find them difficult to read. The borders are illustrated with vignette engravings, what antiquarian map sellers call *carte à figures*: men and women wearing the dress of their native countries; bird's-eye views of London and Par-is; the Sun and Mercury and Venus clad as Greek gods; sea serpents and sailing ships and Neptunes astride dolphins roiling empty map seas. But these maps, despite their fanciful drawings, are not toys. They are Mercator projections, a type of map in common use today. The proportions are wrong: Europe and North America and the Black Sea are too large; Africa and Asia and the Medi-terranean too small; and although I find this troubling, acculturated as I am to the proportions of contemporary maps, I also appreciate that they are real tools steeped in real geography. Drafted during the Age of Discovery, for travelers or for those who aspired to travel, they testify, it seems to me, to the best in our human spirit, to our curiosity, to our desire to see what lies beyond the next mountain or across the next river or over the restive sea.

My mother often complained that what my father had asked her to find on a map "simply wasn't there." Not the number of miles to the next Nevada town. Not the altitude of Donner Pass. From my post in the backseat of the family station wagon, I knew the information Father wanted *was* on the map.

But I dreaded his sarcasm and Mother's anger. So much so that when I reached junior high school, I took over map-reading, to quell their arguments, but also because I shared my father's love of maps. My father and I understood map reading was an art, but an art with rules. You read a map "north up" regardless of the direction you were traveling—failure to do so led to confusion as surely as plague followed Old-Testament sin. You anticipated what came next by identifying (and communicating to the driver) what intersection or street or town preceded the next turn. You always called out the towns and villages that lay down the next branch in the road in the event that a highway route number was unposted. But most of all, you never lost sight of the cardinal directions—north, south, east, and west—thereby bridging the abstraction of the map to the reality of the world. Now, years later, my father gone, I sometimes wonder if map reading was something that he and I were born with, that perhaps not everybody is born with, that compelled us to know where we were as compulsively as a Monarch butterfly must navigate from Manitoba to Mexico, or a salmon from the ocean to its natal river.

Scale, grid, and sphericity define the modern map. Babylonians developed scale; the Chinese, grids. Ancient Greeks added sphericity. Aristotle (384–322 BCE) came up with his famous triple observations for why the world must be round. *Wasn't the lunar eclipse always circular? Didn't ships seem to sink below the horizon as they sailed from view? Weren't some stars visible only from some places on the earth?* Logically, he concluded, the earth had to be round. Where Aristotle argued logic, Eratosthenes (275–195 BCE), the third Chief Librarian of Alexandria, did the math. By comparing the length of two shadows at two different points at a known distance from each other at the summer solstice (when observers at both points would know it was the same time), he calculated the difference in angle between the two points and thus derived the circumference of the earth, with considerable accuracy as it turned out, although probably also with a little luck. Eratosthenes went on to develop a system of imaginary lines—north–south meridians, and east–west parallels, which he centered on the city of Rhodes, similar to our own coordinate system, which centers on Greenwich, England. Two centuries later, Ptolemy, the "father of European geography," made his own circumferential calculation. Where Eratosthenes' circumference was more accurate, Ptolemy's (90–168 CE) survived beyond antiquity. It was Ptolemy's map that led Columbus to conclude that he could make it to India by sailing west. (If Columbus had known Eratosthenes's larger—and more accurate—circumference, he might never have sailed. If Columbus hadn't sailed, Spain might have had no empire. Without the Spanish Empire, the Americas might never have been European.) But despite Ptolemy's erroneous circumference, he gave us latitude, longitude, scale, legends, north up, east right all in the same map. One map. The complete story. What we expect in maps today.

In writing this essay, I paged though my *Rand McNally Road Atlas*, the 2007 edition, where I found a map of the Grand Canyon. On the map, the canyon tracks through green and beige blocks of color: Lake Mead on its lower left; Lake Powell and Glen Canyon at its upper right. By convention north is up. The colors are convention too: blue for bodies of water, dark green for national parks, pea green for lesser monuments like the Vermillion Cliffs. I have visited the canyon a number of times and these colors don't describe the landscape anymore than a Beethoven score describes the Ninth Symphony. The real canyon is a tumult of color: umbers and oranges and grays; pinks and beiges; the high ridges in summer black with Douglas fir and piñon pine, in winter laced white with snowfall. The Vermillion Cliffs are not green but vermillion. In fact, there's almost no green. Little blue either, except the sky. The Colorado River, blue on the map, is no more than a greenish, sometimes muddy red streak snaking the canyon's floor. But we accept these map untruths, parks green and rivers blue, because it helps us understand context. We intuitively feel that "blue" means water, that "green" means park, and that the intensity of the green tells us where the park fits in a hierarchy of parks. By other conventions, the escarpments of the mountains and mesas, the Grand Wash and Hurricane Cliffs and the Shiwits and Kanab Plateaus, are shaded as though the sun is shining from the northwest. None of this tells what the canyon really looks like. We don't see its pinnacles and hoodoos and towers; its sandstone striations; the fossil footprints of amphibians and dinosaurs and trilobites. A map is no portrait: it is symbology, like the treble clef or a hieroglyph; it's a high-brain function, a *Homo sapiens*-defining trait.

On the *Atlas* map of Arizona, with my finger, I trace the highways that approach the Grand Canyon National Park: red for US 89, black for Arizona 64. The traces trigger memories. 1996. A rented RV. My wife Susan, our then-five-year-old son John, and John's nanny, Vilma. We are singing along with Annie Lennox who is singing to us from the RV stereo.

Nowadays maps still reflect the zeitgeist. In our age of hyper-functionality and super-specialization, maps have evolved to highly specific purposes. There are hydrographic, topographic, political, relief, petroleum, precinct-voter, and subway maps. There are maps that chart the sediments that lie invisible under the earth. There are maps that mark its magnetic anomalies. There are maps to track the Magellanic Clouds; the births and deaths of stars; the transits of comets about the sun; the migrations of caribou and timber wolves and grizzly bears. There are maps that track the DNA trail left by our ancestors' perambulations. There are maps that document the trafficking in sex slaves, the warming of the earth, the melting of Arctic ice, the routes used by cocaine smugglers, the marches of army ants, the incidences of Ebola. Drawn in the sand, folded into your jacket pocket, captured in the binary arithmetic of your computer, there are maps that plot the path to the neighborhood 7-Eleven, the course of the Milky Way, the number of burglaries in your neighborhood, where you've been, and where you intend to go.

But because the world has three dimensions and not two, because the earth is ellipsoid and not a perfect sphere, because it's more like a basketball flattened on its top and bottom, because ellipsoids defy ready mathematical definition, because a map's reference point, its datum, requires mathematical definition, even contemporary cartographers face traditional map dilemmas.

A cartographer can hold direction true, or depict the correct relative size of continents, or preserve local scale, or make the distance scale constant in any direction. But he or she cannot hold all these true at once. Fixing one distorts another. In the Mercator projection of the earth—the projection we most often see in our classrooms—Greenland appears to be bigger than South America. An egregious error that occurs because the longitude lines are held equidistant, equator to pole, expanding the apparent size of what is mapped, as the map moves pole-ward. Yet despite this, the Mercator is highly useful, a favorite of mariners because a straight line plotted on a Mercator projection marks the shortest distance between two points, a handy attribute if you're plotting a sea voyage. We pick the projection suited for the purpose we intend.

The ellipsoid (rather than spheroid) shape of our planet creates other problems. Every map must be referenced to a common point. This point is called a map's datum. But an ellipsoid planet offers no simple, common mathematical formula to calculate a datum. Thus there are hundreds of different types of map datums. Some have evolved by historical accident, some have been deliberately obscured to confuse potential invaders, both commercial and military. Some assume the earth is flat; others that only a part of the earth is flat. Some center on the earth's core, others on its surface topology. Each serves a specific need: surveying roads, searching for oil, plotting the course of a ballistic missile. None represent the world as it truly is because all introduce errors. An error of plus-or-minus fifty feet may be insignificant if you are navigating from San Francisco to Chicago. But if you're a scuba diver in murky water at the base of a North Sea oil rig, fifty feet may be the difference between drowning and staying alive. Not surprisingly, this plethora of datums creates confusion. My friend, Josh Hoyt, a onetime Woods Hole oceanographer, tells of a rendezvous that his research ship attempted in the Atlantic with a French research ship. Scientific crews. Experienced captains. The ships could not find each other. Finally the crews determined that of their two sets of charts, each ship had used a chart with a different map datum.

Maps serve more than just utilitarian purposes. Maps also launch our flights of fantasy, enrich our dreams, embellish our tales. One of my favorite boyhood books, Robert Louis Stevenson's *Treasure Island*, begins with a map. Long John Silver. Skeleton Island. Spyglass Hill. Who can forget the X that marks the buried-treasure spot? After I read *Treasure Island*, I began to draw my own treasure maps, imaginary islands with mountain ranges and harbors and rivers and secret trails that wound through swaths of forest, skirted swamps, bridged cataracts, avoided encampments of hostile natives. I particularly liked to draw rivers: you never knew what lay beyond the next bend. I no longer remember what purpose I had in mind, other than to create a place where, like Stevenson, I might imagine my own adventures. Or perhaps I created my maps in a Genesis spirit, where it was I, not God, who dawned light on a new world. No matter. For me, maps enrich a story; they are part of humankind's ongoing narrative, the journeys they record (or offer us) having their beginnings and middles and ends. Without its maps, Tolkien's Middle Earth might lose some of its wonder. Without its maps, Peter Pan's Never Never Land might be less eternal. Without its maps, the movie *Casablanca*, might suggest less context for the plight of a conquered Europe.

Most journeys aren't fanciful. On this particular journey, the one that I'm remembering now, my wife Susan, our then-high-school-junior son John, and I are traveling along Colorado's Front Range, west of Denver, east of the Continental Divide. John sits in the back seat, a notebook computer on his lap, a Garmin 76sc Global Positioning System in his hand. The Garmin is black plastic, three-times the size of a cell phone. Its small screen shows a map of metropolitan Denver as well as our current location southwest of the city. Earlier, before we left home, I generated a computer route from Denver's Stapleton Airport to our hotel and on to three colleges John plans to visit. Now, because of rush-hour traffic, it's up to John to improve our route. John zooms in, zooms out, declutters the screen: he leaves out the local Marriott Hotels, the Conoco gas stations, the burial site of Buffalo Bill Cody. Finally John and the Garmin recommend a route: we will depart Interstate 25 and follow Colorado 470, another freeway that tracks west around Denver. These technologies enchant me: the computer latent with information; the satellites spinning overhead. I like to envision them, a human-built mandala, singing a guiding message.

My Garmin 76sc speaks to my inner nerd. Whether I'm in Piccadilly Square or Italy's Amalfi Coast or British Columbia's Inside Passage, I press a button, wait a few seconds, and voila!, my 76sc tells me where I am. What's more, using different memory cards, my 76sc will display different maps: Blue Chart for nautical navigation, Topo for hiking and biking, City Search for urban travel.

My 76sc is a climax of technologies, part of an exquisite construction of receivers, satellites, ground stations, and monitoring systems that only the most advanced and highly organized society could have brought into being. At least twenty-four satellites in six different orbital planes whirl above the planet. At any time, from anywhere on the planet's surface, given an unobstructed view of the sky, a receiver can "see" at least eight satellites. Each transmits a signal on at least two wavelength frequencies. Ground stations in Hawaii, Kwajalein, Ascension Island, Diego Garcia, and Colorado update the satellites. Each satellite carries an atomic clock so sensitive that it compensates for Einstein's special and general theories of relativity. Every satellite knows not only its own ever-changing orbit and its own "health" but also the expected orbits of its sister satellites. My Garmin 76sc must know many of these facts too, or be able to find them. In its thumbnail-size memory, it holds a satellite almanac and ephemeris that, if printed, would fill a bookshelf. The math the system uses is conceptually simple: satellite distance equals the time of signal transmission multiplied by the speed of signal transmission. But because the speed of transmission is the speed of light, even the smallest difference in time can generate enormous errors. Hence atomic clocks. Hence compensations for relativity; for something called the Sagnac effect, based on the effect the earth's rotation has on the speed of electricity in earthbound clocks; for solar storms, ionospheric interference, and radio-wave scattering; for buildings, trees, and radio and TV transmissions. Year by year, meticulous engineering refines errors out of the system. I purchased my first GPS receiver in 1992. Since then I have purchased two more handhelds, one tiny GPS the size of a fifty-cent piece that plugs into my laptop, two "fixed" receivers for our sailboat, one that came with our Volkswagen Touareg. Each new generation of GPS stunningly improves over its predecessors.

An age has dawned when we needn't be lost. A few years ago, when my son John hiked into the wilderness of north central Alaska, his destination a place called Misery Lake (a name, as it turned out, eponymous with the weather that summer), he took with him his Garmin Rhino GPS. John was a hundred miles from the nearest village, but he knew his location to within thirty feet. The GPS seemed to shrink Alaska. But Alaska's shrinkage was an illusion. If one of John's party had broken a leg or suffered food poisoning or bled uncontrollably, it would have taken hours to mount a rescue. Still, we're talking hours; once we would have talked days.

If an age has dawned when we needn't be lost, it's also true that, if we wish to get lost, we may find it more difficult. Cell phones can track our kids but they also betray our own whereabouts. What would TV police procedurals do without the familiar plot device where bad guys reveal their malfeasances by an ill-considered cell phone call? In the recent movie, *Into the Wild*, based on a true story, the protagonist Christopher McCandless goes to considerable (and ultimately fatal) lengths to jump the grid, abandoning his car in a Utah desert, removing its license plates, throwing away his charge cards so that his parents and everybody else he knows won't know where he is. Ultimately he hitchhikes to Alaska where he meets his end in an abandoned school bus, dead from food poisoning and starvation. Although mostly I like to know where I am—otherwise why have I bought so many GPSs?—there's a part of me that connects with McCandless. Years ago, during college and again when I was thirty, I made two solo trips to Europe. I remember the exhilaration of realizing that nobody knew where I was. Not my parents. Not my ex-wife. Not my then-girl-friends. I was lonely. But I was free.

Our ancestors must have quailed at the words *terra incognita* inked or type-set on a map. Yet the boldest still answered the call: enter where it is forbidden; vanquish what is unknown. But what happens when the empty areas fill in? Do we lose part of what it means to be human?

There is on the dining room wall of our house in Friday Harbor in Washington's San Juan Islands a framed map, a standard NOAA navigational chart titled "Strait of Juan de Fuca to Strait of Georgia." It describes the confluence of the two named straits, which, as it happens, is also the situation of the one hundred ninety-two islands and islets that form the San Juan Island archipelago. The chart colors are understated: tan for the land, white for the deeper waters, a robin's-egg blue for shoal water less than ten fathoms, a muddy olive for areas that dry at low tide. An even paler blue marks the traffic separation zones that keep the big container ships and tankers from running into each other on their way to Vancouver in British Columbia or Seattle in south Puget Sound. Black grids mark the streets of Victoria on Vancouver Island and Anacortes and Bellingham in the United States, but black lines also signify isobars of elevation, the isobars so close together on the slopes of Mount Constitution on Orcas Island that the chart is almost solidly black. The chart, first published in 1907 and little changed in the last hundred years, is a tool rather than a work of art, but I find it beautiful; islands I have known since I was a boy, resonant with memories. Their shapes are so familiar to me that I see them as Rorschach images: Orcas, with its three big harbors, is for me an upside down Dadaist trident; Cypress, where I made my first island landfall in 1958, Casper the Friendly Ghost; Lopez, a rabbit; San Juan Island, a rooster with its feet at Cattle Point, its tale at the peninsula marked by Turn Point and Pear Point, its full breast the "West Side" running from Eagle Cove to Kanaka Bay to Limekiln Point, its beak and cockscomb at Roche Harbor. Memories attach to so many of the named ports, passages, bays, and anchorages that I have an anecdote for almost each name. In Sydney, just across the dotted purple line that marks the US–Canada border, Susan joined me on my boat in August 1980, kicking off a relationship that led to marriage, our son John, and (recently) sending John off to college. We sailed three different sailboats in these islands, dropped wallets and cameras overboard, dragged anchors, savored sunsets, and suffered rainstorms. In Prevost and Deer Harbors, in Echo and Blind Bays, in West and East Sounds, at Jones Island and Turn Island, and Spencer Spit. In 1992 we fell so in love with a small house on the east shore of Friday Harbor that we bought it and still own it and have, for the past fifteen years, commuted here on weekends, taking the ferry or our own speedboat from Anacortes across Rosario Strait, through Thatcher Pass, into Lopez Sound, down Upright Channel, until we arrive in Friday Harbor. I can almost navigate the route with my eyes closed. Still, when I look at the chart, I'm always surprised to find a name or two I never knew or have long forgotten: Picnic Cove, Iceberg Island, Canoe Island. In this I see another manifestation of maps. They track our histories, trigger our memories, mark the boundaries of the places we call home.

If it is good to remember the best things in life, if it is also good to allow the worst to fall away, there are some catastrophes so terrible they must never be forgotten. In 2007 *The New York Times* reported that a French Catholic priest, Father Patrick Desbois, is mapping the graves of Holocaust-massacre victims in the Ukraine. From 1941 to 1944, the Nazis slaughtered 1.5 million Ukrainian Jews. Because the Jews were killed by guns, the slaughter is called the "Holocaust of Bullets." The sites are unmarked—bullets leave no brick crematoria. On a tour to the Ukraine in 2002, Father Desbois asked the mayor of Rava-Ruska where the Jews were buried. The mayor said he didn't know. "I knew that 10,000 Jews had been killed there," Father Desbois told the *Times*, "so it was impossible that he didn't know." The priest resolved to interview eyewitnesses—when the massacres took place, most were children. He travels with two interpreters, a photographer, a cameraman, a ballistics specialist, and an expert on maps. So far the team has mapped 600 sites, having covered only one-third of Ukrainian territory. "People talk as if these things happened yesterday, as if sixty years didn't exist," Father Desbois told the *Times*. "Some ask, 'Why are you coming so late? We have been waiting for you.'"

Maps help us find our way home. Maps help us do our jobs. Maps help us remember our joys. Maps help us remember what we must never forget.

But what if we had maps that charted our interior geographies?

What if there were maps that showed the path to a loved one's heart, maps that marked the exits from a bad relationship to a good one, maps that helped us find the grace to forgive, maps that led us out from the wilderness of Alzheimer's, maps that showed how to bridge the chasms of ultimate regret? What if there were maps to the mysteries that lie hidden in the byways of our hearts?

What if there were maps that warned us, *Here be dragons that might steal your soul?*

In 1960 my father fulfilled his passion to visit Europe. During our five-week visit, he rarely got us lost. But Paris confounded him with its practice of street names changing every few blocks, a problem exacerbated when my father rented a car and my mother became map reader, and also because President Eisenhower and Premier Khrushchev were in town for what would become the failed U2-spy-plane summit. I recall a sun-sweetened May morning on our way from our Bois de Boulogne campground to the Eiffel Tower when my father made a wrong turn. We careened two revolutions around the Place de Le Concorde traveling against traffic, the gendarmes waving their arms and blowing their whistles, the other drivers honking their horns in Gallic disdain, while my father bellowed out our rental car window, *Cuidado! Cuidado!*, Portuguese for "Take care! Take care!," because my father spoke Portuguese and believed that one Romance language was more or less interchangeable for another, an assumption that would bewilder various French, Swiss, Italians, and even Germans over the next few weeks, and that would embarrass me, his eldest son. Nonetheless, from the Bois de Boulogne to the grassy schoolyard-cum-campground south of Dijon where we awoke from our tent amid a curious crowd of French schoolchildren, from Lausanne on Lake Geneva to Bologna in central Italy where my brothers and sister and I first saw fireflies, from the Roman Coliseum to the Carrera beachside campground where my mother suggested that the marble fragments in the sand under our tent floor, so uncomfortable as we tried to sleep, might be fragments of the marble that ultimately became Michelangelo's *David*, from Genoa to Turin and back to Paris, my father guided us with his Michelin maps and his carefully marked routes and in doing so he left a legacy for his children that is as valuable and as imperishable (at least in our own lives) as is *David's* marble.

After my father retired, he bought a sailboat, and our roles reversed. I became guide, he follower. He often told me that he would never attempt the long passages we made into British Columbia had I not been present. I led in my boat and my father followed and I tried to keep him always in sight but sometimes the wind was too perfect and Susan and I would pop open the spinnaker and our boat, *Margaritaville*, would take off and my father in his boat, *Vela*, could not keep up.

Occasionally I turn up my father's old maps: Puget Sound charts, coffee-stained and penciled with nautical transits, Des Moines to Point-No-Point, Point-No-Point to Foul Weather Bluff. Or one of his oil-company road maps from the 1950s, the routes of our family vacation trips traveling the American West: Yellowstone, Yosemite, and Devils Tower; Mesa Verde, Crater Lake, and Craters of the Moon. I always stop what I'm doing to muse over them, to be carried back to the voyages and road trips we made and to be reminded how much I miss him, and to recognize how my own love for maps and my love for my father have twined together. And this, at least for me, is the loveliest gift from maps: when maps bring back the past as crisp as a snapshot, as descriptive as a postcard, when maps seem to say, *the weather is fine, wish you were here*, so, in a way, I always am.

My Tahoe

"Certain places seem to exist mainly because someone has written about them."
—Joan Didion

"Every time I put my line in the water I said a Hail Mary and every time I said a Hail Mary I caught a fish."
—Fredo Corleone, *The Godfather, Part 2*

Blue

WHEN I REMEMBER LAKE TAHOE I remember its extraordinary blue, like cobalt, only bluer, and I remember its clarity and I remember how the rocks twenty-feet down seemed as if they were just beyond arms reach, and I remember the orange bark of the campground sugar pines and the sandy "grus" soil of our campsite and I remember how the lake in July was still too chilly for swimming. It was 1959 when I first saw the lake and I remember being disappointed. The tourist-tacky towns Stateline, Tahoe City, and Truckee; the casinos on the Nevada side of the lake with their tawdry neon; the strip malls with their burger joints, supermarkets, and gift shops; incongruous with what I expected. What I expected was nature predominant. I expected the gold standard, which was the National Parks, where, even when development was tolerated—and it was in Yellowstone and Yosemite and the Grand Canyon, the most visited parks—it was development within the constraints of what the Park Service considered good taste. No neon. No garish colors. No slot machines. There was beauty in Tahoe. But it was beauty compromised.

Later, significant events in my life would play out in this place.

Later, more than beauty would be compromised.

* * *

Tahoe Redux

After my family's first visit in 1959, I didn't visit Tahoe again until 1974. After that, not until 1978. After that, not until the late eighties and early nineties. During each of these visits, history accumulated, though I made no attempt to connect it. As I grew older, however, I became interested in the tie between place and one's history. Were there patterns? Were some places consistently associated with joy and others with trouble? Did place shape events? Or was it the other way around? Did memories shape subsequent events in the same way that ancient archeology is sometimes dug up and dusted off and used to justify the present?

Lake Tahoe, it seemed to me, was one of those places. A place of beauty. But also of ambivalence.

In 2009, I resolved to visit Tahoe again. I planned to search for lost memories, undiscovered epiphanies, and unrecognized confirmations, to determine whether my memory of Tahoe has been hostage to reality or hostage to myth. To remember what it was I didn't want to forget. To determine whether Tahoe's ambivalence was endemic to Tahoe. Or endemic to me.

Forgiving and Forgetting

Lake Tahoe is a place my wife Susan might suggest I forget.

Susan accuses me of never forgiving; I think Susan confuses forgiving and forgetting. But Susan is right to counsel against the perils of the past. The past is never definitive. It has a tendency to mutate to what wasn't there. Still, if we tolerate forgetting, don't we risk losing what *shouldn't* be forgotten? And isn't life too transitory to forget anything? And if we forget, don't we lose part of what makes us who we are?

Whatever the case, Lake Tahoe is a place I can't forget.

Where my first marriage unofficially ended. Where a corporate career began its decline.

The Lake in Its Place

If you trace the California–Nevada border, starting at the Oregon state line, the border plunges due south until about the latitude of Carson City, the state capitol of Nevada, at which point it darts southeast still in a straight line along the east flank of the Sierra Nevada Mountains, clipping Death Valley National Park, crossing the Mojave Desert, until it intersects the Colorado River not far from Lake Havasu, Arizona. The point where the border suddenly departs southeast, near Carson City, is the location of Lake Tahoe.

The lake straddles the Sierra Nevada Mountain Crest. Due east is the site of the Comstock Silver Lode and Virginia City, the silver-mining town made famous by Mark Twain in his wild-west memoir, *Roughing It*. Due north is Donner Pass, the site of the infamous Donner Party's cannibalistic winter encampment. Due west is California's Gold Rush country.

The lake is twenty-two miles long and twelve miles wide with seventy-two miles of shoreline. At 6,225 feet elevation, it's the largest alpine lake on the continent. It has a maximum depth of 1,645 feet, making it the third-deepest lake in North America (Crater Lake, in Oregon, and Great Slave Lake, in Canada are deeper). It is so deep that its lakebed floor is lower than the Carson Valley to its east in Nevada, where Reno is, and where, via the Truckee River, the lake's sole outlet drains into landlocked Pyramid Lake, a "chemical sink" according to the Keep Tahoe Blue website, which, like the other lakes in the Great Basin—the vast, high stretch of land that's mostly in Nevada and western Utah—doesn't drain to the ocean. Sixty-three streams and small rivers plus direct rainfall and snowfall feed the lake. The streams and rivers are snowmelt and are why the lake has such extraordinary clarity, even if the clarity, under pressure from human development, has diminished for the last fifty years. It's a lot of water. If the lake were to empty tomorrow, refilling it would be a labor of time: given normal precipitation, it would take six hundred years.

Still, there are a lot of North American lakes bigger than Tahoe. The lake's modest size surprises me. Perhaps because events here figure large in my life.

A Riddle

We forget it, we manipulate it, we exaggerate it, we distort it, we forgive it, we blame it, we seek it, we lose it, we search for it, we hide from it, we learn from it, we intuit it, we study it, we inherit it, we live in it, we run from it, we love it, we hate it, we rewrite it, we long for it, we eulogize it, we worship it, we justify it, we curse it, we fear it, we return to it, we rediscover it, we repeat it.

What is it?

The past.

A Question

If we don't reexamine the past, how do we know where our stories truly begin?

A Short Story

Early in my writing career I set a short story at Lake Tahoe. The story was about a young couple estranged from each other. The wife invites the husband to visit her and the husband sees her invitation as a gesture of reconciliation. The wife has actually invited him to negotiate a divorce. While the husband is staying in the wife's rented ski condo, there are a number of phone calls. When the husband answers, the callers hang up. On the second evening, when the wife is out (she claims to have a job as a bartender), two men—are they police or criminals?—knock on the door. They ask for the wife and "her husband." But the real husband realizes they're not asking for him. His suspicions aroused, the real husband searches the condo and discovers that his wife and the false husband have been dealing cocaine, and that some of the supply is stored in the condo. Worried that the sinister men might return, the husband begins to flush the cocaine down a toilet. While doing this, he discovers a box of prophylactics. Concluding that the prophylactics illuminate his wife's infidelity, he fills the prophylactics with the remaining cocaine and tosses them one by one off the condo porch into the snow. Then he gets in his car and drives away. Here the story ends.

When this story was critiqued by members of my writing group, one woman judged it unrealistic. "No man," she advised, "would be so vengeful."

The Godfather

The Godfather: Part II is the darkest of the *Godfather* movie trilogy. The movie opens in a scene at Lake Tahoe. Where the first *Godfather* is about family and loyalty to family and can be said to extol such virtues beyond its mafioso mayhem, *Part II* is about the price that malfeasance ultimately demands. In the movie's opening scene the Corleone family celebrates a first-communion party for Michael's son. The scene is shot at the family compound on Lake Tahoe, the sun bright, the partygoers colorfully clad, the lake the purest of blues. As *Part II* progresses, Michael Corleone, played by Al Pacino, seems to sink into himself; his eyes and cheeks hollow out, his features grow darker, betrayal follows betrayal, blood engenders blood until even the cinematography darkens. In the next-to-last scene, Michael watches from a boathouse as his minions execute his brother, Fredo, an execution that Michael himself has ordered. Now the lake is black and gray and sinister, its purity corrupted by what the story has revealed, by what Michael Corleone has lost, by what the Corleone family has lost, but also, perhaps, by what all America has lost.

Which view is the true view of Tahoe?

Light or darkness or something of both?

Seismic Certainty

The geology that created Lake Tahoe is *block faulting*—the block below the lake dropped down, those on either side uplifted—the same geology that shapes the basin and range topography of Nevada all the way to the Rocky Mountains, and that partly formed the Sierra Nevada Mountains to the west and the Carson Range to the east. The two ranges are distinct. The Sierras are a jagged, ice-cut topography of alpine glaciation, while the Carson Range is rounded and gentle. This is because the Sierras, during the last Ice Age, blocked the moisture-laden storms rolling in from the Pacific Ocean, thus precluding the snowfall essential for Carson Range glaciers. Several of the Sierra-side glaciers terminated in the lake, forming features like Emerald Bay, a glacial cirque within the lake. The lake itself, however, was not carved by glaciers, although during the Ice Age, it was filled with bergs.

The orogeny that uplifted the Sierra Nevada has ended. The Sierras have begun their epochal process of being worn down, as the Appalachians have been worn down, but the area is still seismically active. A network of down-to-the-east faults fractures the Tahoe basin: the West Tahoe-Dollar Point fault; the Stateline/North Tahoe fault; the Incline Village fault. About 1500 CE, a magnitude 7-plus paleoquake generated a lake-borne *seiche* (what a tsunami on a lake is called) that swept Tahoe with waves more than thirty feet in height. Another seiche will happen. It's a seismic certainty.

Mining Memories

It's 2009 and Susan and I have driven down from Seattle, have picked up our son at his university in Santa Clara—John has just completed his freshman year—and now the three of us have proceeded east across the Central Valley and ascended the Sierra Nevada foothills. This is Gold Rush country. Placer, Amador, and Calaveras Counties. Diamond Springs, Angel's Camp, Sutter Creek. I see something weary in the land, as if the miners' took away more than gold. In any case, gold shaped this place; the placer hydraulic mining technology blasted hills into creek beds. The scars one hundred fifty years later still stain the earth. In a way, what the miners have done here is what I intend to do with Tahoe: mine it for memories.

Gold Rush country is also retiree country.

At the Placerville supermarket, where we stop to stock up on provisions, there are several oldsters pushing wheeled walkers and sucking oxygen from rolling canisters. Do they seem wearier than most retirees? Maybe I'm seeing what I want to see, the people as tired as the land. Maybe they're at peace. Maybe they're at last savoring the golden years for which they so long labored. But maybe their weariness is real.

After we leave Placerville, the highway begins to ascend the Sierra Nevada Mountains. This is how you get to Lake Tahoe. It's how Californians have gotten to Lake Tahoe for one hundred fifty years. The American River flows free and clear here, and US 50 parallels the original wagon track from Sacramento to Tahoe. Manzanita forest gives way to tall, straight Douglas fir and orange-barked lodgepole pine. We pass the Kirkwood Ski Resort where a chainsaw artist has sculpted a wooden bear. We spot cell phone towers constructed to look like trees—orange-brown towers, fake limbs and boughs; something, we decide, that's essentially Californian.

The drive is beautiful: the river below us, the conifers sweetening the air, the car humming into the turns and accelerating out of them.

Is there something about California that inspires automobile marketing: *Malibu, Sonoma, Bel Air, Sequoia, Mojave, Sierra, Catalina, Monterey,* all names for automobile models. Perhaps it's because nobody loves their cars more than Californians. Perhaps because the rest of America likes to imagine itself on California's highways. Perhaps because the idea of California is inseparable from cars. Perhaps because nowhere else in the world do so many highways offer so many magnificent drives.

Whatever it is, my first SUV—a gas-guzzling behemoth—was called a Chevrolet *Tahoe.*

I loved my Tahoe.

But as we approach the lake, I feel anxiety. I've been to Tahoe a number of times but this time, for the first time, I've set out to deliberately mine its memories, to dig into the archaeology of my Lake Tahoe past.

The First Peoples

The Washoe people inhabited the Tahoe basin for hundreds of years. Tahoe's etymology derives from their word, *da wa,* thought to mean "big lake." When the European-Americans arrived, in typical Eurocentric fashion, they named the lake Bigler, in honor of John Bigler, a southerner and the first governor of the State of California, an eponym advocated by such luminaries as Mark Twain (although Twain's advocacy may have been sarcastic). The name "Tahoe" first appears on an 1862 Department of the Interior map in lieu of "Bigler," because Bigler, a Confederate sympathizer, was persona non grata on a map published during the American Civil War by the Union government. Well into the next century, both names were used and it was not until 1945 that "Lake Tahoe" was officially adopted. The Washoe people fared less well. Faced with the onslaught of European, Chinese, and African-American miners, railroad builders, farmers, shopkeepers, and innkeepers, the Washoe found themselves derided as "diggers" and were soon displaced from their ancestral home, another instance in the sad history of European-American and Native-American relations, California being a particularly despicable chapter. The Washoe name for Tahoe endured. The Washoe people, at least in the Lake Tahoe Basin, did not.

Cannibals and Dreamers

The first European-Americans to see Lake Tahoe were John C. Fremont and his scout, Kit Carson. The date was February 14, 1844. Fremont didn't stick around, but he played a minor role in another famous episode of Tahoe's history.

In the late fall of 1846, at Sutter's Fort in California, James Reed, leader of a group of immigrants stranded in the Sierra Nevada Mountains, begged Fremont to organize a rescue mission. The group included Reed's family. Fremont, then a US Army colonel, was unable to help, his hands full with the Mexican War. The group came to be known as the Donner-Reed Party. It would not be until February that a rescue team reached the stranded immigrants. By then the grisly cannibalism, for which the Donner-Reed Party is infamous, had begun. Of the eighty-seven people who had begun the trek in Utah's Wasatch Mountains, forty-eight survived. The survivors never escaped the approbation their cannibalism engendered. (The California writer, Joan Didion's, great-great-great grandmother, Nancy Hardin Cornwall, narrowly missed being part of the Donner-Reed party; her ancestor's people, traveling with the Donners as far as the Humboldt Basin, opted for a different, safer, non-desert-and-high-Sierra route north, toward Oregon's Klamath River.)

What strikes me about the Donner-Reed Party is how ill-prepared they were: Illinois farmers, small-town merchants, European immigrants, they lacked the skills to navigate a continental wilderness but set out anyway, impulsively, hopefully, recklessly, foreshadowing the hundreds of thousands of other California immigrants who would follow and whose dreams would be, more often than not, just as blind.

Tourism

The first Tahoe resorts dated from the 1860s to accommodate the Comstock Lode silver miners in nearby Virginia City, only twenty or so miles east of the lake. As early as the turn of the twentieth century, wealthy Northern Californians had begun building homes on the lake. By the 1920s, the building boom had begun that continues to this day. There was a mansion built to resemble a Viking castle. Michael Milken, the 1980s junk bond impresario, post-prison, had a home on Lake Tahoe. Henry Kaiser, the aluminum baron and the founder of Kaiser Motors built his compound named Fleur du Lac, the site chosen as the set for *The Godfather: Part II.* (In true Hollywood fashion, the compound, supposedly located in Nevada, is actually in California, and the background mountains are the Carson Range, not the Sierra Nevada.) Today Fleur du Lac is mostly torn down, replaced by a condominium development. Each boom and bust cycle has spawned a new wave of multimillionaires and faux-chalets.

Most of the lake is not so exclusive. In Tahoe City, on the California side of the lake, you can find all the trappings of outdoor tourism: bike rentals, boat rentals, kayak tours, river-raft trips; boat-launching ramps, postcard shops, inflatable beach toys, gas stations, public beaches, water skiers, jet skis, bikini-clad (in-season) bathers. The bridge over the Truckee River, the lake's sole outlet, is locally known as "the Fanny Bridge" for the taillight views of what the *The New York Times* travel magazine calls "the Great American Backsides"—tourists peering into the diamond-clear river, their backs facing the bridge traffic. Tahoe's Nevada-side resorts go back much longer than legalized gambling. But the essential tourist character of the place, it seems to me, especially for those who are not winter-sports enthusiasts, is shaped by gambling.

An Old Mafia Lodge

Robert Stone begins his wonderful, dark, short story, "Bear and His Daughter," in a Lake Tahoe casino, where Smart, the alcoholic poet/protagonist is slugging down whiskeys in, as Stone calls it, "an old Mafia lodge on the north shore of the lake." As the story unfolds, Smart hits a winning streak while shooting craps in the casino, becomes increasingly drunk, gets involved in an altercation with the pit boss, and is ultimately escorted out of the establishment by its security staff. Smart wakes in his car the next morning in the hotel parking lot and stumbles down to the shore of the lake following a trail. The scene closes as Smart lies on a rock and drinks directly from the lake so as to ease the pain of his hangover. The trail, he muses, is almost like backcountry wilderness, except for the fact that "The hotel was not the sort where guests took walks in the woods."

Kool Inside

I'm not a gambler. I have an aversion to gambling, likely due to my mother who heaped scorn on all casinos and all casino customers, on every supermarket and café slot machine we sighted during our family vacation transits through Nevada. In most cafés, a row of slot machines was ubiquitous near every cash register (if the cafés were air conditioned, a penguin sticker adorned their glass doors, the penguin blowing smoke rings, under which the Kool brand of cigarette's slogan "*It's Kool Inside!*" was inscribed). But gambling, casino gambling, just as it is most other places where it's legal, has become an essential star in the constellation of Tahoe's firmament.

The "gaming industry," as its proponents call it, is a pastime toward which Americans have a schizophrenic regard. Sometimes we tolerate it. Sometimes we proscribe it. Nevada welcomes it. Nevada legalized casino gambling in 1931, attracting a round of Tahoe casino owners with names like "Bones" and "Wingy." Tahoe didn't reach its gambling zenith, however, until the early 1960s when Frank Sinatra purchased the Cal-Neva Hotel and Casino and luminaries like Marilyn Monroe and, it was rumored, the Kennedys (Jack and Bobby), followed secret tunnels to liaisons in luxury bungalows. Sinatra's tenure was short-lived—on entertaining a mobster-friend, Sam Giancana, (whose girlfriend was also a Kennedy mistress), at the Cal-Neva, Sinatra lost his Nevada gaming license. "Old Blue Eyes" had to sell the place, which subsequently began a slow, geriatric decline. The tunnels and the bungalows are still there; so is the Cal-Neva; the Nevada State History website denies the presence of any Kennedys.

Jet Lag

Can we be so predisposed against a place that what happens there only serves to confirm our predispositions?

At the Incline Village Hyatt, in Nevada, on the northeast shore of Tahoe, it's nearly impossible to get from one place to another without passing through the hotel casino. During my business-meeting stays in this hotel in the late eighties and early nineties (at the time I was one of the vice presidents of a California computer company), I unsuccessfully sought routes that avoided the casino. The idea behind these events was "relationship building." We were to get to know each other—all the attendees were vice presidents or directors—through scavenger hunts, wine-and-cheese tastings, round-table discussions. Make allies, was the watchword. I ignored this advice. I was based in Hong Kong. I was jet lagged. It addled me to walk and it addled me to sleep, and it addled me to open my mouth to speak and it addled me to close it and listen. I had no allies, I sought no allies, I thought I needed no allies.

My boss booked us into tacky rooms in a tacky hotel with a tacky casino and promised, with a wink and a nudge, not to schedule meetings too early the next morning. How incongruous it was: the blue lake, the Sierra Nevada Mountains, the stands of pine outside the door while most guests, including my boss and most of my executive peers, immersed themselves in an artificial night. Regardless of the hour—breakfast time, cocktail hour, midnight—the casino was busy. The green baize tables, the spotlight lamps over the blackjack players, the ponging, clattering, chittering cacophony of slot machines and roulette wheels, the cave-like darkness of the cavernous room, the cocktail waitresses in their short skirts and low-cut blouses, the watered-down drinks, the croupiers with green eyeshade visors and dry, vacant faces, the dearth of anything that bespoke nature—no sunlight, no starlight, no plants, no birdsong, nothing to remind the patrons that an indigo lake lay outside the casino walls.

During one of these events, my Hong Kong secretary, Hedy Chu, booked me a day early into the hotel. (Hedy was worried I wasn't getting enough exercise or rest). But I didn't know I'd arrived a day early. I wandered around the hotel trying to find my meeting. Conference room after conference room was empty. Was I in the wrong hotel? Had I arrived the wrong week? When I asked the desk clerks, they stared back at me blankly, perhaps assuming that I, like Robert Stone's poet Smart, was just another drunken gambler, lost, in their casino. *If you've been invited to a meeting, shouldn't you know where your meeting is?* Finally, I spotted my boss, his peers, and my boss's boss sitting around a table in one of the smaller conference rooms. I exchanged greetings, pulled up a chair, and plopped into it. After a minute or so of awkward talk, the European Sales VP leaned over and whispered that I'd interrupted a private meeting. (My own boss, somewhat cynically, allowed me to babble on). As it turned out, my boss's boss had just announced, the minute before I sat down, that he'd been fired. His successor was a highly popular female vice president whom I didn't know but whom I'd noticed at these events enthroned in the cocktail lounges, surrounded by fawning surrogates. Her appointment would eventually raise a storm that would sweep me up in it. At the time, however, I was just embarrassed. I sought respite jogging on a path laid between the hotel and the lake, not unlike Robert Stone's "wilderness trail." My jog, wobbled by jet lag, was antidote to embarrassment. Looking back, the day was a turning point. Events skipped into motion spinning lives, my own included, onto different tracks, into another story, a story that deserves its own time and its own place even if that time and place aren't here or now.

But back then, I couldn't see it.

Snow

What, besides the lake and gambling and mountains, is Tahoe's signature characteristic?

Snow. Four hundred fifty inches annually. Seven ski resorts. Thousands of feet of mountain vertical.

When Squaw Valley, the most famous of the Tahoe ski resorts, bid for the 1960 Winter Olympics—the year was 1955—there was no mayor, one chairlift, two rope tows, one small fifty-room hotel, and a single, fulltime inhabitant. When the US Olympic Committee submitted their Squaw Valley bid, Avery Brundage, the famously authoritarian International Olympic Committee head, was reputed to have said, "the USOC [United States Olympic Committee] obviously has taken leave of their senses." But this was another America. An

America with less red tape. An America where California still worked. An America where people said if you wanted to see the future, go to California. Five feverish years later, the ski runs, ice rinks, speed-skating tracks, ski jumps, hotels, and freeways were in place. It was an Olympics of firsts: the first Olympic Village to house all the athletes together; the first appearance of the modern Olympic torch; the first Olympics pageant produced by Walt Disney (four thousand singing children, two thousand doves); the first Olympics to be televised; the first to use what would become TV instant replay; the first competitive use of metal skis; the first Winter Olympics outside Europe post-WWII; the first Olympics in the United States post-WWII; the first to tabulate results with a digital computer (IBM). There's something quintessentially Californian in this luring of the Olympics to an untested venue, one without highways, hotels, and ski lifts, something you might expect from a place that specializes in spectacle, that celebrates hustle and chutzpa and self-actualization, Californian characteristics that have been partly lost.

What do you do in the winter here if you don't ski in Tahoe?

You shovel snow.

And it was snow, not gambling, that attracted me to Tahoe.

Novice

The second time I skied at Tahoe, I came with a woman I'd been dating in San Diego. She'd graduated from a college in Colorado and she'd told me (or I thought she'd told me) that she was an expert skier. On our first morning on the mountain, we launched ourselves down an intermediate run. She fell and she got up and she fell again and she never admitted anything and she never apologized for anything and she never explained her novice skiing and she never admonished herself and she never admonished me and she never acted embarrassed and for this I came to appreciate her even more.

Golden Land

The Chinese name for America is *mei guo*, "Golden Land." After the discovery of gold, the trickle of immigrants to California, only a thousand or so a year at the time of the Donner-Reed Party, swelled to a torrent. After the gold played out, Nevada's Comstock Lode, just east of Lake Tahoe, drew another wave, this time of silver miners, among them a former Mississippi river pilot, Confederate Army deserter, and would-be miner named Sam Clemens. Later, under his nom de plume of Mark Twain, Clemens would go on to immortalize (and fantasize) the American western experience in his memoir, *Roughing It.* The lake entranced Clemens. "So singularly clear was the water," Clemens wrote, "that when it was twenty or thirty feet deep the bottom was so perfectly distinct that the boat seemed to be floating in air!"

John Muir, the environmentalist, who famously described the Sierra Nevada Mountains as the "Range of Light," was appalled that the Tahoe lakeshore had been deforested in order to supply scaffolding for the shafts and tunnels of Nevada's mines, but he too marveled at the lake's extraordinary blue. "As we look from the head of Emerald Bay," Muir wrote in his journal, "the distant mountains are blue and the lake is blue, with exactly the same tone, and the yellow summer sky is like the glow of the desert beyond the mountain-rim."[1]

Travelers and pamphleteers have continued to praise the lake's blue. They often cite its multitude of hues. All speak of its clarity. But in the fifty years since the lake's clarity has been routinely measured, it has declined by a third.

Tahoe's waters are clear, but it's a clearness imperiled.

The Keep Tahoe Blue initiative has brought together two states, disparate federal agencies, a half-dozen municipalities, environmentalists, and developers to study the causes of lake pollution, to slow its advance, and to hatch a plan to ultimately reverse it. The process is astonishingly complex, partly because the original clarity was so high, partly because the elements that contribute to clarity are so numerous. Nitrogen from vehicle exhaust, phosphorous from road dust and natural forest emissions, ash from wood stoves and condo fireplaces, sediment from storm-sewer runoff, soil from ski runs, dirt roads, and campgrounds, erosion from stream-channel watercourses no longer filtered by natural wetlands, all of these feed the lake's algal biomass or add to its suspended solids.

Algae and dirt are the cause. But human activities are the culprits.

---

1 Linnie Marsh Wolfe, ed., *John of the Mountains: The Unpublished Journals of John Muir,* (Madison: University of Wisconsin Press, 1979), 286.

Still there's hope, there's commitment, and there's modest progress. Tahoe may yet stay blue.

Sugar Pine Point

John, Susan, and I have arrived at the southern end of the lake. We turn west and north on California Route 89 following the Sierra Nevada shore. I've chosen Sugar Pine Point State Park as our night's destination. We're low on fuel. Should we turn back? I decide to proceed.

We can't see the lake because of stands of conifers and the fenced-and-gated lakeside estates. Route 89 narrows and rises and winds through glacially carved granite. John Muir's Range-of-Light granite. We're rounding Emerald Bay, the glacial cirque within the lake, in which, on an island, rises the Scandinavian castle known as Vikingsholm. We can't see the castle. We do glimpse the lake. Slate blue. White granite. Green pines. Stony. Silent. A fitting setting for a Norse saga. Route 89 drops back down into the trees. Emerald Bay and Vikingsholm vanish behind us.

The Sugar Pine Point campground is set well back from the shore and on the opposite side of the highway. Five leisurely campground loops, two plywood-sided buildings housing flush toilets per loop, a half-dozen water spigots, a handful of RVs parked on asphalt plots, two or three fellow tent campers, a cast-iron grill for campfires, a bear-proof locker for food, a concrete table at each site, a whiff of campfire smoke, the whine of the first evening mosquitoes, the tang of OFF!, the crack of an ax splitting wood, the peen of our hammers against our tent pegs, the sandy, pine-needled earth outside the tent, the gray, soft, satin light filtering through the trees. It's the first week of June, a Thursday, and Sugar Pine Point is *nearly empty*.

Susan prepares a salad and marinates three steaks. John and I build a campfire. We barbeque the steaks on our portable propane grill. The fire warms us. The air is sweet with pine smoke. Sparks ascend a starry sky. Still, in the back of my mind I can't help thinking: what snowbound was to the Donner Party, logging to Muir, Hyman Roth to Michael Corleone, the Nevada Gaming Commission to Sinatra, Tahoe is to me.

Snow—The Prequel

The first time I skied Tahoe was in 1974. My estranged then-wife, V, invited me to visit her at the condo she was subletting. She had taken a job as a Squaw Valley ski-lift operator during what she called "our trial separation." I could stay with her, she suggested, and get in some skiing. She added that she missed me and that she looked forward to seeing me and to catching up on my news. It was thirteen months after the Paris Peace Accords, nine months after my navy ship, the USS *Enterprise*, had come home from Vietnam (the same homecoming day V told me she was thinking about a divorce), and six months after V left me for her "trial separation."

We'd lost the war (even if those of us in the military still wouldn't admit it). The first Arab oil embargo had begun. The country was suffering through Watergate. The whole nation seemed exhausted. On the *Enterprise*, I was one of the engineers who operated and maintained the ship's nuclear power plants, a demanding and never-ending job. I drove up I-80 toward the Sierra summit, husbanding the gas in my little yellow sports car. Fifty was the new speed limit. My anxiety grew as the distance between Tahoe and me shrunk. Had I been daft to accept V's invitation? Had I been daft to hope to win her back? At Donner Pass, I turned south, following V's directions.

V's condo wasn't far from the lake. It was set back in a stand of sugar pines. Shadows slatted a one-lane drive that snaked back into the trees and amid the condo clusters. Mounds of snow lay under the pines and the mounds glittered in the afternoon sunlight as if they were silver and gold. The air was pure and clear. In the face of such clarity my anxiety faded. I was filled with optimism and I was filled with hope.

V had left a note on the door. She would be back in time for dinner, all I had to do was turn on the oven. The dinner she'd prepared was a favorite of mine—mock *cordon bleu*. When V arrived, we embraced and she placed her hand on my elbow but I could feel her stiffen as we kissed. That night we slept in the same bed. Her perfume—I no longer remember its name—was gardenia-scented, and it reminded me of Chesapeake Bay summer evenings when V and I first dated, dusky, damp, vanilla-sweet, sexy.

We didn't make love.

The next day V asked me to have lunch with her. I met her at her chairlift. At lunch, on a sun-warmed, open-air deck, amid happy skiers, she handed me a book. The book was titled *Do-It-Yourself Divorce.* Later that year, whenever I closed my eyes, I would see her chairlift. Later that year, each night before I fell asleep, I would see her book.

That afternoon, I skied runs marked double-black diamond, whose steepness alone should have deterred me. I skied runs beyond my skill in the hope that skiing them, no matter how often I fell, would restore a degree of control over my life. But I didn't enjoy it.

That evening with V, I spoke of our future together; V spoke of divvying up our rugs.

I'd wanted reconciliation; I'd wanted us together; I didn't get what I'd wanted.

Collateral Damage

In divorce, damage is often collateral. Eight months elapsed before our divorce was final. But the marriage ended at Tahoe. The monumental misapprehension between V and me might have occurred anywhere. But it occurred here. At Lake Tahoe. We had no children and we had no money and we were married only three years, but much was lost. My innocence, my optimism, my faith in love and reasonableness was lost; the good times I remembered with V, now tainted by discord and divorce, were lost. Most of all youth was lost. If there's a moment I mark as its end, it's here, at Lake Tahoe, perhaps before its time.

Maybe V was more prescient than I. Maybe she saw our future incompatibilities: her ties to Maryland gentility, her tolerance for Annapolis Bull-Roast politics, her love for horses and English-style riding; my shyness, my abiding Northwestern-ness, my love for mountains and boats. I understand how a young woman can assess her life, decide the course is one she wished she hadn't chosen, and then set a new course.

But understanding isn't forgiving.

V was careless with me and it's her carelessness I find difficult to forgive.

She would return to vex me again, not at Lake Tahoe, a year and a half later but only for a few months, and by then I should have known better, and perhaps I did. I didn't offer so much of myself the second time around.

But, later, with other women, I offered less of myself too.

Some couples divorce and stay friends; others never speak. V and I never spoke.

Questions with Some Answers

For life to be lived to its fullest, must the future contain the past?

Yes.

All the past? Or just some of it?

I don't know.

Heartbreak

Each year at Lake Tahoe there's a boat show called the *Concours d' Elegance*. You wouldn't expect a wooden boat regatta on a mile-high lake but the boats are here: Chris-Crafts and Hacker-Crafts and Gar Woods gleaming in mahogany glory. I love wooden boats. I love them because like people, they're perishable, they demand love, and they benefit from attention. As it turns out, the environment at Lake Tahoe is well suited to wooden boats. The lake water is fresh without the deleterious effects saltwater has on varnish. The climate is the right balance between moisture and humidity. And the boats, most manufactured prior to World War II, were already here, playthings of California's pre-WWII elite. In *The Godfather: Part II*, on the night the Miami gangster Hyman Roth sends his thugs to assassinate Michael Corleone, an assassination made possible by the treason of Michael's brother, Fredo, it's wooden boats like these—Chris-Crafts, Hacker-Crafts, and Gar Woods—that speed frantically back and forth in the dark lake off Fleur du Lac searching for the assassins.

Later in Havana, after Michael confirms Fredo's treason, he grabs his brother by the head with both hands. "I know it was you, Fredo," he says. "You broke my heart."

Questions Without Answers

Are forgiveness and forgetting mostly the same? Must we forget to forgive? Can we live a moral life, do the right thing, love our spouses, be kind to our children, be content in our present life without forgiving events in our past?

Runners

We break camp early at Sugar Pine Point. The morning is cool. The sky thinly overcast. Today we'll circumnavigate the rest of the lake and then we'll pick up US 50 again, drop down into Carson City, and continue our trip across Nevada on the highway *LIFE* magazine once christened "the loneliest road in America." The boat moorings along the shore are empty; in June, at this altitude, it's still early for boats. The Fanny Bridge at Tahoe City is empty too; the tourists must still be scarfing down hotcakes larded in butter and lathered in syrup. The lakeshore road is bordered on one side by small homes and on the other by a path, and, as we proceed into Nevada, the path begins to fill, at first with solitary runners, and then with runners in groups of twos or threes, and then with groups of dozens of runners, and then with elderly runners, and then with runners who are walking rather than running, and then with runners who are limping and finally with runners' families, friends, and fans. The Nevada State Park along the shore is stunning—rock formations, islets, emerald-green coves—but, because of the runners, there's no room to park the car.

Clues and Portents

In our garage at our vacation house in Friday Harbor on Washington's San Juan Island, I still have the navy sea chest issued to me when I was a midshipman at the Naval Academy. The chest is a plywood box with a hinged top and a lockable hasp. It has followed me around the world and it holds the detritus of previous lives: service dress blue uniforms, tropical dress whites, gold buttons, black-felt shoulder boards, medals, letters of commendation, snapshots, Kodachrome slides, wire-binder journals with felt-tip entries blurred beyond discerning, June Week dance pictures, a naval officer's ceremonial sword, navy coffee mugs, plaster-of-Paris ship's plaques, a photo of the *Enterprise* autographed by the ship's captain. I've been reluctant to discard this stuff. It's all that remains of two decades of my life, even if it has meaning only to me. There are clues here to who I was, to who I was going to become, to who I am. One is a portent, a photo of V: she's sitting at the bottom of a series of stone steps; along one side, ascending the steps, is a flower market; the flowers are red and blue and yellow and they are displayed under green umbrellas; the steps are on Hollywood Road on Victoria Island in Hong Kong. The photo was taken in 1972, at the end of my first ship's Vietnam deployment. For years this photo was important to me. Not because of V. Because of Hong Kong. It contained elements that fascinated me: the symbiosis of Asia and Europe; colonialism meeting the East, side streets and side beauties within a teeming metropolis. I remember telling V as we climbed these steps. "I could live here."

And fifteen years later, in another life, with another wife, I did.

Lake Blues and No Portents

John, Susan, and I have reached the junction of Nevada 28 and US 50. We have turned east and Lake Tahoe has vanished behind us. We've spent less than twenty-four hours here.

I came to look for the past.

What have I found?

Of my ex-spouse and my last, miserable weekend with her, of my former non-skiing girlfriend and her unflappable cheer, of those jet-lagged corporate scavenger hunts, of my humiliation before my boss and his peers, of the clanging, clattering cacophony of the casino, of the remora-like sycophants who circled my future boss in her Squaw Valley cocktail-lounge soirées, I've found no physical trace.

Where were the former bosses, ex-wife, and long-since-gone girlfriend? Not here.

Wherever they are, they weren't here.

And I've found no portents.

What I found were pine-scented campgrounds, a campfire warming us against a June evening's chill, a river flowing as clear as diamonds, marathoners and speed walkers circling the lake, and a lake so blue with aquamarines, indigos, and turquoises, that it seemed to hold all the blues in the world.

My Redwoods

I FIRST SAW THE REDWOODS IN 1950. My family had just toured Yosemite and San Francisco. We were on our way home. I don't remember much (I was only three years old). I remember a saw-cut trunk, its girth twice as wide as my father was tall, its growth rings labeled with events from history—the Declaration of Independence, Columbus's voyage to America, the Magna Carta. I remember my mother explaining that this tree, the one she and I were touching, had been older than Jesus. Even then, even at three, I knew something that old was old indeed.

The redwoods are old, some as old as three thousand years. We know the earth evolved from stardust and once-living things—comets and coral reefs and Cretaceous ferns—and we know it's not eternal, but by the daunting enormity of its years, it seems eternal. The coast redwoods are old in a different sense: they are old on a scale we comprehend. Maybe because monuments raised by human hands—the Pantheon, Westminster Abbey—began to be built when a living redwood we can see and touch was already a hundred feet tall. Maybe the fact that the trees lived when our ancestors lived makes our ancestors somehow less dead. Or is it a kinship we recognize with all life, a sense that we and the trees are of the same cloth?

They say to know a place you must let its soil become your bones, its seasons fall upon you, its winds chill you, its rains dampen you, its droughts parch you; you must watch its clouds sail overhead and mark its dawns, listen to its crickets, suffer its gales, savor its fragrances, recoil from its stenches, touch its rocks and trees and grasses, warm your feet in its sands. They say you must live in a place to know it. But I don't believe this. I have in my sixty-some years driven through the redwoods and walked through the redwoods and camped in the redwoods and changed my son's diapers under the redwoods and watched my mother change my brothers' diapers under the redwoods, and yet in all that time I've spent less than sixty hours in the redwoods. But the redwoods shape me, are always with me, anchor me to the sacredness of life. Some places take time to inhabit. Others inhabit you the moment you see them.

The oldest redwoods were saplings before the first brick was laid for the Parthenon and the Coliseum, before Chartres Cathedral or the Hagia Sophia Mosque in Istanbul, before Fontainebleau, and (probably) before the Great Wall of China. The oldest are older than Christianity, Islam, Hinduism, Buddhism, and Baha'i. They have outlasted the Roman Empire, thirteen Chinese dynasties, what was supposed to have been Hitler's thousand-year Reich. The oldest have lived long enough to become the tallest trees in the world, to become (along with their Sierra sequoia cousins) the trees with the largest arboreal mass, and to become, next to the gnarled and weather-beaten bristlecone pine, the second-oldest living things on the planet.

Redwoods are also among the oldest species of trees. Their kind has survived longer than the woolly mammoth, the cave bear, and the giant ground sloth; they have survived the polar ice that seventeen times since the dawn of their kind crept down from the poles; survived the clash of tectonic plates that periodically rattles the California coast; survived the rise and fall of oceans; survived volcanic eruptions that turned summers into winter; survived the comet crash that killed the dinosaurs.

They are uniquely suited to survive. Their bark is thick and spongy and inures them to fire. During rainless summers they trap moisture from fog. The tannins in their bark repel insects. They survive flooding rivers—the Chatco, the Trinity, the Klamath, the Smith—because their roots, unlike other species', know how to grow up. They survive despite seeds that are as small as tomato seeds; despite relying on the wind to pollinate them; despite germinating less than one percent of those seeds and despite less than one percent of those germinated becoming seedlings. They survive because they are monoecious, meaning they have separate male and female flowers and do not require the pollen or seeds from another redwood; they survive because, if no seed germinates, new saplings will sprout from fallen trunks forming rings that are called *fairy rings* (a term I love for its folkloric beauty).

Redwoods have survived the arrival of Native Americans, the Spanish Conquistadors, and the Russian fur traders. They may not, however, survive the gold prospectors, railroad tycoons, loggers, the backyard-deck builders who call themselves Americans. Unfortunately for redwoods, their wood is an ideal building material. It doesn't shrink, warp, cup, decay, absorb finishes, leak resins, or combust easily. Buildings are said to have survived the San Francisco earthquake and fire solely because they were constructed of redwood. This has led to a conflict between lumbermen and environmentalists that has lasted a century and which, by its lack of resolution, leaves the survival of old-growth redwoods in doubt.

If we lose the old-growth redwoods, we may pay a higher price than aesthetics. While the Pacific Ocean tempers the cold, sends the wet-season rain, moderates the summer heat, eases with its fog the dry-season drought, and thus creates an ideal environment for redwoods, recent studies suggest that an old-growth redwood forest shapes its own environment by harvesting water directly from the atmosphere through "fog drip," which in turn augments the aquifer, which in turn fills the streams, which in the turn provides pure clear water for, among other plants and animals, the endangered Northern California salmon runs.

You kill the redwoods, it turns out, you kill the salmon.

* * *

As an adult living in California, I often found myself in the redwoods, especially, it seemed, when change was sweeping my life.

I found myself in redwoods during the dissolution of a first marriage. A weekend dawned when I could no longer deny its collapse. I set out on a solitary drive up Highway 101 from San Francisco. The highway was endless and my back ached and my hands numbed and I fell into a torpor in which I saw everything and saw nothing. When I reached the redwoods I stopped at a roadside park. The day was gray and gloomy. It had begun to rain. Redwoods rose in dark, dense groves on either side of the road, their spired crowns broken by winter storms, the bases of their trunks charred by fire. To my surprise, as I sat at the picnic table and sipped a Dixie cup of cheap California cabernet, it occurred to me that these broken and burned giants offered a note of hope: that life outlasts travail; that much could be said for simply weathering the storm.

I found myself in the redwoods again in April 1979, the month I got out of the navy. I'd driven from Washington State down US 101 south, bound for a new, if uncertain life as a civilian. Before you reach the Oregon–California border, US 101 flirts with the ocean. It edges away at the Chatco River, kisses the coast again at the border, then skitters inland along the Smith River. The sky blazed blue. Wildflowers dappled the median. Douglas fir lined the highway. But I hadn't seen any redwoods. Then a dense stand ahead loomed over lesser trees as if the redwoods were mitered bishops presiding over bent acolytes. I stopped the car and set off on foot through the grove. What I felt then was what I'd felt before and would feel again: a reverence similar to what you experience in the great cathedrals of Europe. Light falls in the same soft-slatted way, as if it had passed through a clerestory window, trunks rise straight and true like piers in a nave, the boughs dome like arches. The trees spire up; your spirits lift; you're closer to whatever it is that causes such beauty to exist. And how could it be otherwise? Isn't a redwood grove—solemn, silent, sweet-scented—God's true chapel?

Twelve years later, married a second time and with our one-year-old son John, I passed through the redwoods with my young family. We'd just returned to America after six years in Hong Kong and, though our life in Asia had been exciting and financially rewarding, we'd begun to miss snow-clad mountains and the cool, clean American Pacific Ocean and the breathing room of the American West. In the press of our trans-Pacific move, however, packing, leaving old jobs, beginning new ones, showing off our new son to grandparents, siblings, and old friends, we'd fallen into a state of exhaustion and ennui. Baby John was throwing up. His nanny Vilma had the flu. My wife Susan and I were suffering summer colds. Our homecoming drive had turned into an ordeal rather than a celebration. After a sleepless night in Coos Bay, Oregon, we crossed into California and stopped for a picnic lunch along the Redwoods Highway. The July sun that only minutes before glared off the highway was now softened by redwood boughs, and the stale air of our van gave way to the clean, camphor scent of the redwood forest, and as the redwoods rose above us, they seemed to shelter us, and for the first time since we'd returned home, I felt as if we'd finally come home. It seemed not only that the redwoods welcomed us but that during all our time in Asia they had been here, a lodestone calling us back, and now, at this change in our lives, we were here again. Was it accident? Or was it destiny?

* * *

The year I'm remembering now, my son John is eleven years old. We're camped on the banks of the Smith River in California's Jedediah Smith Redwoods State Park. John skips stones across the Smith, which runs fast and clear here. Across the river a forest rises: Douglas fir, western hemlock, big leaf maples, laurels, alder, tanoak, sorrel. Of course redwoods. We see their trunks, some red, some tan, some gray—the color varies because redwood color genes have evolved over such a long time that they have a larger-than-other-species variety. The understory is dense. I wonder if it's possible to even walk through it: salal, huckleberry, thimbleberry, sword ferns, rhododendron, and azaleas crowd each other in profusion. Not far from us, perhaps less than ten miles away, are the tallest redwoods on the planet. The park officials keep the location a secret (they fear vandalism) but in this rugged country even a redwood can hide. I don't need to see them, the tallest of the redwoods. What brings me here is the whole forest, from the lichen on the forest floor to the great canopy above us with its hanging gardens and miniature groves invisible from the ground that I'll never see. What brings me here is continuity. What brings me here is that I've been here before. What brings me here is that in this place I feel a reverence for life. What brings me here is that this is an ancient and holy place.

John holds up a flat, river-polished pebble.

"Call it," I say.

"Five." He slings the rock sidearm. One, two, three, four. . . . The rock sinks. He shakes his head, shoots me a sheepish look.

I pick up my stone—black, the size of a silver dollar. Where was it born? In the fire of a volcano? The icy core of a comet? "At least five," I say. I wind up and let it rip. One, two, three, four—it's still going—nine, ten, eleven, twelve. The rock slides underwater. In a second, the current erases every trace. "Don't worry," I say. "You get better when you get older."

"Like right, Dad."

"Race you to camp?"

John takes off, his feet kicking up gravel. He'll win this race.

But perhaps what I said was true. Maybe age does make you better. Maybe practice can lead to perfection. Maybe time teaches. Or maybe in the presence of old things you slow down, fall silent, listen, until at last you can hear the steady, soft, imperceptible heartbeat of the universe.

Ice

Some say the world will end in fire,
Some say in ice.
—Robert Frost

M Y MISSOURI-BORN GRANDMOTHER, Catherine Seybolt, widow of a
Methodist clergyman, liked to confirm the Bible through geology—the
Flood, the Parting of the Red Sea, how Jesus could be seen to walk on water.
Her agnostic son-in-law, my father, John Mathison, abetted Grandmother's
interest, but for his own secular reasons, bringing forth account after account
in which natural phenomena explained apparent miracles: fossils atop Mount
Ararat; how under certain meteorological conditions the Red Sea actually part-
ed; or places in the Sea of Galilee so shallow that you might look as if you were
walking on water.

Grandmother was less concerned with the reality of miracles than with
how phenomena might be seen as miracle. She believed the Bible was metaphor, but metaphor based on actual events: what its authors saw and then
struggled to interpret. Later I would recognize this as a sophisticated view. Back
then, however, when I tried to do the same, I gave it up, concluding that what
I saw in my native Northwest defied Biblical explanation. The ice-crowned
Cascade and Olympics peaks, Puget Sound's deep channels with their racing
tides, the volcanic fields and the flood-cut coulee canyons and petrified forests
of central Washington, all represented a geological truth more potent and more
ancient than anything in the Bible. Here tectonic plates clashed. Plate-borne
continents rammed one another. Once-living mollusks deposited themselves in
long-gone seas—and then actually turned to stone! Here a furious volcanism
raised mountains and, much more recently, a mere blink of the eye by geological reckoning, continental ice laid flat the earth and then carved it up again.

In the face of such geology, how could you attribute mere miracles?

* * *

My home state's ice-shaped geography originated from the great continental glaciations, the Cordillera Ice Sheets that four times in the last two million years invaded Puget Sound. (Of course, the ice wasn't invading Puget Sound, as much as it was making Puget Sound.) At the height of the most recent Fraser-Wisconsin Ice Age, 75,000 to 10,000 years past, three-fifths of all the ice in the world lay in North America. Its southernmost extensions were the Juan de Fuca and Vashon lobes, which reached into what is now Washington.

Looking at Puget Sound from the perspective of geographical foreknowledge, the effects of the ice seem obvious. But it wasn't until the nineteenth century that geologists began to appreciate how much ice had shaped the world, as John McPhee so cogently explains in his collection of essays, *Annals of a Former World,* which first appeared in *The New Yorker,* and which introduced to many non-geologists like me the newest ideas of contemporary geology.

In 1795, James Hutton, a Scot, speculated that certain gravels and boulders in the lower Swiss valleys might have been carried there by extensive ice (but he missed the evidence of ice that had shaped his own native Scotland—*eskars,* the long, serpent-like ridges of sand and gravel deposited by streams flowing under glaciers; *drumlins,* the thin ridges left in the wake of a moving glacier; and *erratics,* the boulders deposited by melting glaciers, all of which laid the groundwork for what would become the prototype landscape for the world's golf courses). I love these words—eskars, drumlins, erratics—that seem to hearken of Norse sagas. Some years later a Swiss, an initially skeptical Jean de Charpentier, also concluded that many geographical features in Switzerland could only be explained by ice. When in 1836 a young medical doctor, Jean Louis Rodolphe Agassiz, rented a cabin up the road from Charpentier in the alpine Rhône River Valley, Agassiz, under Charpentier's tutelage, soon recognized that ice had indeed shaped the valley. In 1837 he published his *Époque Glacier,* a thesis of continental glaciation that was greeted with derision. Even Agassiz's mentor, the famed geologist Alexander von Humboldt, counseled his protégé that his obsession with ice might endanger his career: ". . . your ice," von Humbolt wrote, "frightens me."

* * *

It seems to me that ice age glaciers grew in ways similar to how the scientific zeitgeist sometimes evolves. Or perhaps zeitgeist is too large a word. Theory is more like it. The accumulations of precipitation, lower temperatures, and the net winter-to-winter gain in snowfall that causes the ice to spread is akin to what happens when, little by little, an apostasy—an idea that challenges established dogma—transforms to dogma itself. The ice had an inevitability about it, a shifting restlessness, a self-reinforcing momentum.

* * *

The causes of ice ages are still speculative: the uplift of the Rockies and the Andes and the Himalayas and the Alps—the great orogeny of plate tectonics—may have cooled the climate for the last sixty million years; or volcanic ash may have reflected the sun's energy back into space; or the weathering of mountains may have brought on a chemical reaction that removes carbon dioxide from the atmosphere, a sort of reverse greenhouse effect; or the wobble of the earth's axis may have tilted in just such a way as to increase the cooling; or the sun may have reduced its energy output.

But, because in the four-billion-year history of the planet an ice age phenomenon is so rare, it's likely a collusion of these.

* * *

At the maximum advance of the last great continental ice sheet, all of Canada lay below thousands of feet of ice. At Bellingham in Washington State, just south of the British Columbia border, where short-story writer Tobias Wolf sets his lovely snow-laced short story "Powder," the ice was over six thousand feet deep. At Seattle, it was five times deeper than the six-hundred-foot Space Needle is high. At Tenino, south of the state capital Olympia, where the ice sheet terminated, a torrent of melt water coursed south and then west entering the Pacific Ocean at Grays Harbor and Willipa Bay. In the Olympic Mountains, ice deposited Canadian boulders at what is now 4,500 feet. It left sediment over a thousand feet deep on both sides of the fjord that demarks the Olympic Peninsula from Puget Sound and which is called Hood Canal. It left glacial kames, kettles, drumlins, and bogs at Port Angeles. It left eskars and lateral moraines on Whidbey Island. It left the gravel that forms most Puget Sound beaches. When the ice began to melt, it released so much weight from the earth's crust that for the next thousand years the land rebounded until it had risen five hundred feet at Seattle and eight hundred feet at Whidbey Island, just thirty miles north of Seattle; the land rose faster than the sea, which was also rising from melting ice—you can still see the wave-cut traces of previous shorelines hundreds of feet above the present Whidbey Island beaches.

From Cape Flattery on the Pacific coast to Olympia to the British Columbia border, with the exception of the two great mountain ranges that frame Puget Sound (these shaped by their own alpine glacier systems), the geology we see today is a geography of ice.

* * *

Officially the ice age is still on, although we're in an interglacial hiatus, or an interstade, as geologists name it. The most recent advance ended only ten thousand to twelve thousand years ago; the next, if the cycles are maintained, will return fifty thousand to one hundred thousand years from now.

We fret about global warming. Should we really fret about the return of ice?

* * *

There are a dozen different molecular structures for ice but only two exist at the temperatures and pressures that support our terrestrial biosphere. Of these, only one is common. The common form is called ice-Ih. It is a kind of hexagon crystal. Imagine it as a Tinkertoy with six planar sides, with wheels as the molecules and pins and spokes as links between them. The hexagon structure of ice is why snowflakes are hexagons. It's less dense than water in its liquid state, thus, ice floats. It's also surprisingly stable: it takes four times the energy to melt ice as it does to melt an equivalent amount of iron, seven times the energy to melt ice as it does to melt an equivalent amount of lead.

Ice is mostly white. Since white reflects the sun's short-wave radiation, ice may help prolong ice ages.

Ice is an effective earthmover. It abrades rock by using the rock it already carries like sandpaper; it also fractures the rock when subglacial water seeps into fissures, freezes, and expands; then the ice plucks up the rock, and transports it away, sometimes for hundreds of miles, explaining why the north side of the Olympic Mountains is laced with British Columbia rock, rock delivered and deposited there by ice.

Ice is slippery, although the mechanism of slipperiness is not fully understood—current theory suggests that slipperiness occurs because ice molecules in contact with air cannot remain in their crystalline state. At very low temperatures, however, as those you might encounter in Antarctica, ice loses its slipperiness. Pulling a sledge through Antarctic snow can be like pulling a sledge through sand.

* * *

Try to imagine a world without ice. No ice to chill our gin and tonics. No ice to give us Peggy Fleming. No Yosemite Valley. No Half Dome. No Lake Superior. No Apollo Ono. No ice hockey. No Redwings. No Bruins. No glacial crevasses and no moraines. No eskars or drumlins or wandering erratic rocks. No snowflakes or hail or frost-whitened mornings. No snowmobiles and no skis. No horse-drawn sleighs. No island of Manhattan. No Puget Sound.

Try to imagine a world with a different kind of ice. What if ice didn't float? What if it wasn't white? What if it froze at a higher or lower temperature? What if it didn't sublimate into vapor? What if, in the biosphere as we experience it, there was more than one kind of common ice? What if ice was other than water? What if our ice was dry? What if ice wasn't slippery? What if ice wasn't cold? What if we had ice in our veins? What if when we wanted to stop a thing all we really had to do was put it on ice?

I find it interesting, perhaps profound, that wherever you go on the earth and, as far as we know, anywhere you go in the universe, ice, at the same temperature and pressure, observes the same rules. Ice is always ice.

The universe didn't have to be a universe of rules.

But it is.

* * *

One of the reasons ice remains so vivid to Puget Sounders is because it's still here. When I was a School Patrolman at McMicken Heights Elementary in the late 1950s, we had to ride our bikes down to Military Road where we posted ourselves as crossing guards. From Military Road we could see Mount Rainier. If you haven't seen "the Mountain," as we natives call it, its immensity is hard to appreciate. It rises from sea level to fourteen thousand feet. Its nearest neighbors are only six thousand feet high. Thus, Rainier appears to stand alone. But it's not the mountain's height or its solitude that impresses. It's the mountain's massive snow-and-ice bulk.

My brother, Charlie, and I spent many summer weekends camping the mountain's campgrounds and hiking its trails and lolling in its alpine meadows: Klapatche Park, Van Trump Park, Summerland, Indian Henry's Hunting Ground. Often we skirted the glaciers, clambering around their dirt-gray snouts and over their powdery moraines and up into their U-shaped valleys. Glacial sounds became familiar to us: the hollow rockfalls, the roar of rivers, the whistle call of alpine-dwelling rodents called marmots. We had merely to pull our caps over our eyes and let our senses float out—to the sounds, to the breezes, to the cold-to-the-touch-and-ice-sculpted rock. Then we envisioned an icier day, a millennia of ice, an age of ice.

The mountain's glaciers have retreated during my lifetime and have grown during my lifetime and some, like the Carbon River Glacier, are still growing, still carving out their valleys, throwing up their moraines, sending their silt-gray rivers into Puget Sound. There is something latent in them, something animate in their ice, something that hints at violence.

* * *

Does place shape how we see the world? Having grown up in the Puget Sound country, and having returned to live here much of my adult life, I like to believe that our geography shaped me and shaped my neighbors: the uplift of mountains signifying a world that always transforms to something new; the tidal refreshing of our bays and estuaries reminding us that so much in the world is renewable; the ice caps glistening on our mountaintops cautioning us that even on the hottest days we live in a world of seasons. I like to think my neighbors share this view although I know we live countless different lives: some watch professional wrestling when I prefer to read a book, others play softball on summer weekends where I will always be sailing, others are violinists in neighborhood orchestras—you may find me waterskiing behind a fast boat. Some scale Cascade peaks. Some kayak rivers. Some even weed their gardens. I wonder: with so much diversity, can my neighbors and I see anything in common?

* * *

The November Monday after JFK was assassinated was a National Day of Mourning. My father took us out on Puget Sound on the family's new, eighteen-foot runabout. We launched the boat from a mainland boathouse at Redondo Beach, opposite Maury Island, one of Puget Sound's bread-loaf islands, "bread-loaf" because it looks like a bread loaf with its clay high-bank shores and its narrow gravel beaches that are characteristic of being shaped by ice. The day was cold and gray. We felt as if the assassination had irreversibly chilled everything. On that day it was easy to imagine what it had been like when the ice was here: cold and bleak and shaping, only this time, on this day, what was being shaped was us.

You mark the events of your life by the places you were when they happened. And the places mark you. You've felt their textures under your bare feet. You've lain on your back and stared at their clouds. You've let their rocks and sand and gravels run through your fingers. You've felt their grasses and seaweeds wrap your ankles. Their sun warmed you. Their rains dampened you. Their breezes chilled you. The places where you grow up are in your bones.

Puget Sound country is only a little more than halfway from the equator to the North Pole. But it feels closer to the pole. Our winters may not be as bitterly cold as Boston or Minneapolis or Fairbanks, but even in the height of summer, you feel the kiss of winter. We're in an ice age, and it's only in abeyance. In a tick of the geological clock, the ice might return.

* * *

My grandmother, Catherine Seybolt, was a woman of faith. Faith in God. Faith in the Women's Christian Temperance Union. Faith in the Right of Women to Vote. Faith in the Methodist Church and the Doxology and the NAACP. Faith that when she died, she would spend the rest of eternity with her husband, William.

I envy Grandmother her eternity with Grandfather William.

But I don't have her faith.

There are times when I despair at the fleetingness of life. A life long enough to ask questions about creation but not long enough to find all the answers. But there are other times when I think that just being able to think about creation, to try to wrap our minds around it, may be enough. In many ways geology is the study of creation and creation is the study of time, a time so vast that bones become stone, sea floors become the highest of mountain summits, continents sail the surface of the earth. I find this saga of creation astonishingly beautiful and deeply reassuring, a creation far more satisfying than a Creationist's creation.

* * *

The late paleontologist, Stephen Jay Gould, wrote that sentient life is unlikely because it's the outcome of too many evolutionary accidents. The dinosaurs, Gould liked to point out, ruled the earth for 240 million years and never, as far as we know, evolved our kind of intelligence, an intelligence that cannot stop asking why, that cannot resist trying to explain why, that demands explanations whether by science or by miracles.

When I walked with my son John down a Puget Sound beach and we spotted shell fragments in a cliff or found agates and jasper in the gravel, my explaining to him why these rocks were here brought me much joy. It was a joy as profound as partaking of a good meal or staying dry at night or having good sex. Our desire to know, to explain things is what makes us different. It's what makes us human beings.

Some anthropologists speculate that without the ice age, humanity might never have honed its desire to know things. The cooler climate transforming the forests of southern Africa to savannas, forcing our ancestors out of their trees, demanding they live by wit rather than climbing skill to escape the predation of their carnivorous enemies.

We are not so much stewards of the world, as the Bible tells us, but stewards of ourselves. Perhaps this is our destiny, if there is such a thing as destiny: to keep the race alive so that the flame of curiosity will keep burning, burning here at least, if not elsewhere in the universe.

Maybe curiosity is as rare as Gould's sentience.

Maybe curiosity approaches the divine.

Maybe without the ice age humanity would never have been curious.

Maybe curiosity *is* the Divine.

* * *

There is a park on the shores of Puget Sound, south of Des Moines, north of Redondo, called Saltwater Park. As a boy I spent many summer afternoons there. It is a place my grandmother, Catherine Seybolt, loved. Even when Grandmother was well into her nineties, my mother brought her there for lunchtime picnics.

As Washington state parks go, the park isn't particularly spectacular. It lies in a ravine that opens onto a beach. The ravine has been shaped by a creek. The creek flows down from what was once a glacial lateral moraine—the sideways wake of gravel pushed up by the glacier's retreat. If you follow the creek to its source, it begins as a notch in the moraine-formed ridge amid vine maple, Oregon grape, wild blackberry, and Douglas fir, then drops down through a campground. From the campground you can wade all the way to the beach. The water is so cold your ankles will turn red. You'll pass under a wooden bridge and then through a corrugated culvert that runs under the park access road. The culvert is dark, damp, and a little scary, just within the tide's reach. Snails crawl up its metal walls. There are periwinkles and crawdads. Streamers of algae and creek grass brush your bare legs. You enter one end in fresh water and you exit the other into saltwater. If you don't watch your step, the barnacles will cut your feet. The beach spreads out in a broad, shallow fan of glacial gravel. It smells of seaweed and mud and iodine. Sea squirts shoot water as high as your waist. If butter clams are in season, and if there's no red tide, you can dig them, although as a boy I never found many. You often will see children wading here (some might even be swimming here), despite the gravel, the cold, the crabs, the currents, and the barnacled rocks.

To the north, toward Des Moines, the beach narrows below a bluff pebbled with glacial till. The bluff is prone to slides. Park officials long ago cut stair-step shelves in an attempt to arrest the slides. Ten thousand years ago the bluff was sediment in a pro-glacial lake that lined the side of the Vashon lobe of the Cordillera glacier. But the berm between the bluff and a riprap seawall is manmade, set with picnic tables and fire pits.

Beyond the seawall, a sandbar extends into Puget Sound.

Across the Sound, you can see Maury Island, with its high clay cliffs ("high-bank waterfront" is what real estate agents call it).

Beyond Maury Island, you can see the Olympic Mountains, a skein of peaks zigzagged like a lightning bolt—even in summer, snowfields and ice whiten their summits.

If you grew up in Maine or Ontario or Oslo, or in upper New York State where my grandmother Catherine spent her teen girlhood, these landforms would be familiar to you. The gravels and silts and rocky beaches. The cold water. The hint of winter that you feel even in August. I don't recall my grandmother mentioning ice in any particular way. But the shape of Puget Sound must have felt like home to her. These are high-latitude places. Places born of the ice. My grandmother grew up in a landscape of ice.

If the land shapes us, shapes how we see the world, shapes how our brains work, in a way, Grandmother was a child of the ice.

As perhaps are we all.

The human race.

Every one of us, a child of the ice.

The Catastrophic Columbia

Stones

Hᴏᴡ ᴅᴏ ᴡᴇ ᴅᴇᴀʟ ᴡɪᴛʜ ᴄᴀᴛᴀsᴛʀᴏᴘʜᴇ? In Japan, in the eighteenth and nineteenth centuries, after tsunamis struck, stones were erected that bore the admonition *Do not build closer to the sea than here.* In Japan's disastrous March 2011 tsunami, the stones accurately forecast the farthest reach of the waves.[2] I find these stones appealing. Erected by ancestors who knew their children and their grandchildren and their grandchildren's children would need advice. A rare instance of foresight, although as it turned out, it was advice mostly ignored.

Not far from where I live, on the Columbia River, in eastern Washington State, catastrophe destroyed, catastrophe created, catastrophe occurred far more frequently than most of us know, or want to know.

Where are *our* stones?

The Umatilla Bridge

My wife Susan, my son John, and I drive several times a year from our home in Seattle to our house in Idaho's Big Wood River Valley. We cross the Columbia River at Umatilla, Oregon.[3] This is desert country; *shrub steppe* biologists call it, dry, rolling terrain where scarps of rock billow up like peaks through a layer of clouds. The outcrops are basalt from Miocene lava flows that poured onto the Columbia Plateau seventeen to fourteen million years ago (with lesser flows up to six million years ago) and that were, subsequently and, in geological terms,

---

2 The stones were accurate despite the barriers that were expected to mitigate the waves.
3 Umatilla is the name of a Native American tribe that lives in the area and of the language spoken by several tribes. It's pronounced pretty much as written: the *u* spoken as "you," the *a's* and the *i* short, the double *l* like any double *l* in English. Like most native peoples, the Umatilla faced their share of catastrophe.

rather recently, stripped of their topsoil by ice age floods. When fallow, the hills are cloaked in dun-colored sagebrush and bitterbrush and bunchgrass; in spring, they turn a delicate green and are dusted sulfur-yellow with arrowleaf balsamroot. The soil is ash from the Cascade and proto-Cascade volcanoes, as well as wind-deposited loess blown here during the ice ages, twelve to fifty thousand years ago, and it's among the most fertile soils in the world. Where I-84 crosses the river, the prevailing wind roils the reach between the bridge and McNary Dam. Here the red and black navigation buoys lean counter to the wind. The current is strong. We often spot sport fisherman in small boats as they troll and jig for Chinook salmon or Columbia River sturgeon. The dam is one of fourteen on the river and one of forty-five in the river's watershed, which includes the Snake River, the Kootenay, the Pend Oreille, the Clark Fork, and the Flathead rivers. In the course of a single generation the dams have moderated these once fast-running courses into a series of sedate (apart from the wind) reservoir lakes. The dams have also devastated the salmon runs and drowned the homes and villages of the native peoples as well as many pioneer farms and ranches. For the natives—the Umatilla, the Sinxt, the Secwepemc, Ktunaxa, Blackfoot, Spokane, Coeur d'Alene, Yakima, Nez Perce, Cayuse, Palaus, Cowlizt, Molala, Klickitat, Wenatchi, Siukiuse, Sanpoil, and Nespelem—the arrival of the European-Americans was catastrophe. Disease, displacement, denial of treaties. But, in a larger sense, the Columbia River and the Columbia Basin have always been geographies of catastrophe. Lava. Volcanoes. Earthquakes. Ice. The greatest floods the world has ever known.

Borders and Boundaries

I have a great affection for rivers. Slow rivers. Fast rivers. Braided rivers. Rivers that loop in lazy oxbow bends. Like a siren's call—enticing, deceptive, at any minute able to leave you high and dry. The great river of my home state is the Columbia. When our son John was younger, on reaching the Umatilla Bridge, Susan and I would demand he name it. We wanted him to know the Columbia as we knew it, a moat to cross, a signifier of adventure, a harbinger for returning home. Most of the time John humored us. "Columbia," he would shout.

From its origin in the Canadian Rockies, the Columbia courses through one Canadian province and two American states. It flows south along the west flank of the Canadian Rockies, crosses the US–Canada border just west of Spokane where it subsumes the Pend Oreille, loops west through Lake Roosevelt, the reservoir formed by Grand Coulee Dam, briefly circles north into the Colville Indian Reservation before it turns south again skirting the east flank of the Cascade Mountains, makes an abrupt eastward bend at Washington's "Tri-Cites" of Richland, Kennewick, and Pasco, where it joins the Snake, and then continues west through the Wallula Gap to the Columbia Gorge and the Cascade Mountains, passes Portland on its southern bank, captures the Willamette, jogs north toward Longview in Washington, and then west again until it enters the Pacific at Astoria on the Oregon–Washington coast. It travels 1,243 miles and, with its tributaries, drains parts of British Columbia, Washington, Idaho, Montana, Utah, Wyoming, and Nevada, a watershed the size of France that spans forested mountains, arid deserts, lush river valleys, rolling uplands, deep gorges, and five American and six Canadian National Parks.

I don't recall when I first became aware of the Columbia, although my parents and I crossed the river in the winter of 1949 when we moved from California to Seattle. Like Mount Rainier and Puget Sound and the Pacific Ocean, the river was something of which I always seemed to be aware. I do recall first seeing its traditional, unofficial headwaters (unofficial because there are too many lakes and streams in the Columbia's watershed to warrant a single "official" source). It was 1953. My parents, my grandmother, and my two brothers and I were trailer-camping to Canada's Banff and Lake Louise Parks on the Rocky Mountain crest at the British Columbia and Alberta border. Three days into the trip my mother noticed a rash on my youngest brother's chest. She diagnosed it as German measles. I remember the hushed conversation as my parents decided whether to continue the vacation or to return home. (A return, for my father, who lived for his summer vacations, would have been a catastrophe, albeit a small one). My parents decided to continue. Within a couple of days all three of us boys had measles. Mother bought us sunglasses with cardboard frames and dark cellophane lenses and quarantined us to the car. We made a day trip from our campground at Lake Louise up along a gravel road that was overshadowed by spruce and pine and fir and dust, dust, dust. Until we reached the Columbia Ice Fields. I remember the ice brilliantly white, even through our sunglasses, and I remember the red snowcat buses that took tourists up on the ice and how my father left us in the car and ventured out onto the ice. Almost fifty years later, Susan, John, and I visited the same fields. By then the road from Lake Louise was paved and renamed the Icefields Parkway, and the ice had retreated from where it had been in 1953; the retreat was identified by markers along a path that led across a dusty moraine. The snout of the glacier was devoid of vegetation, a desolate place, and the ice was gray with silt and less majestic than I remembered it. We saw no red snowcat buses.[4] The headline here, however, was still ice. The headline of the river's recent geology is ice. But the deep time geology of the Columbia, or what would become the Columbia, began hundreds of millions of years ago. Before the ice.

Island Arcs, Deep Time, and the Clash of Continents

Deep time is daunting. You see a long way into it but never to its bottom.

The summer before John graduated from high school, he, Susan, and I made a camping journey across the northern tier of eastern Washington. The area is known as the Okanogan Highlands, and the Columbia River marks its eastern and southern boundaries and the Okanogan River and the Cascade foothills its western border. The region is distinct from the rest of desert Washington. Pine forest. Open meadows. Less sagebrush. A topography serried by mountains and valleys running every which way, not like the north–south lie of the Cascades, or the east–west lie of the anticlinal ridges near Yakima and the Tri-Cities. The Okanogan originated when several island arcs began crashing into North American about two hundred million years ago. I like the phrase "clash of continents." "Clash" conveys a magnitude of violence. Strictly speaking, the arcs were not full continents but micro-continents and the clash occurred at less than a few inches a year, although sometimes, as in the March 2011 Japan earthquake, it must have transpired suddenly and with more immediate consequence.

---

4 I have since read that in the high tourist season from July to August red buses still venture out on the ice, although they are now more advanced than the war-surplus snowcats in service in 1953.

For the last two hundred million years, geology in the Columbia Basin has been violent. When the Atlantic Ocean began to form on the eastern shore of North America, the spreading crust shoved North America west, causing the Pacific floor to dive under North America and drawing several island arcs—essentially like today's Japan, New Zealand, and Indonesia—into North America. As the Okanogan terrane "docked," the North American coastal plain folded and sank into a coastal, oceanic trench, and rose up again forming what is now called the Kootenay arc. The term "docked" implies something orderly and peaceful. What occurred wasn't peaceful: chains of volcanoes; a new ocean trench; magma heating, melting, and transforming to granite; batholiths rising up to the earth's surface like corks popped from champagne bottles. What's more, two more micro-continents were on the way—the North Cascades Terrane and the Insular Terrane. Dinosaurs may well have watched the Okanogan and subsequent micro-continents landing on the North American coast. In a handful of sand, it is said, there are no more than ten thousand grains. How much sand would be two hundred million grains? How many years are two hundred million years? But make no mistake. What began two hundred million years ago continues to this day.

There's something about deep time and about deep time geology that's akin to a creation myth. Like Genesis, or the Hopi world birth legends. These tales comfort us, even when they're fabulist or incomplete. But deep time is not intuitive, not something we feel in our bones. Our lives are too short; we are candle flames, quick to ignite, quick to burn out.

On our Okanogan odyssey John, Susan, and I camp at Kettle Falls, on the eastern shore of Lake Roosevelt, the reservoir lake formed by Grand Coulee Dam. It's an overcast June evening, warm and dry and it's still dusk at 10:00 p.m. and the sky is a pearly white. A fishing tournament is in progress and late into the evening and again in the morning the bass boats, fiberglass, low-slung, their paint glittery and metal-flecked, speed up and down the lake as if they were plastic torpedoes. Each flies a bright green tournament banner. I snap a picture of John sitting in a camp chair in front of our gray, domed tent, John trying to read, waving me away with his hand, annoyed that I've taken his photo, caught in a fragment of time, a few seconds, that's all.

Volcanoes, Fire, and the Flood Basalts

The Columbia Basin's geology is dramatic like grand opera. I didn't always appreciate this. When young we see the familiar as mundane, whether an Empire State Building, a Civil War battlefield, or a bellicose geology.

In the 1950s and early 1960s, when I was a boy, the Interstate Highway System was still being built. Most of the highways from Seattle to the rest of the world were two-lane. The dearth of lanes made us feel isolated, but also exceptional, as if we were living on an unspoiled and unexplored frontier. US 10, the main highway east, was typical: after you crossed the Cascade Mountains at Snoqualmie Pass, US 10 was two-lane all the way to Spokane and, after that, two-lane through Idaho, Montana, and North Dakota until you reached the Twin Cities in Minnesota. Closer at hand, once over the pass, the highway passed through the small railroad and cattle towns of Cle Elum and Ellensburg and then wound down a defile that ended on the Columbia River's western bank. Here the Old Vantage Bridge spanned the river and there was a state park. The park was called Gingko Petrified Forest. In those days, my family vacationed throughout the West and we visited most of its National Parks and National Monuments and I had become inured to the grandiosity of the West, so much so that it seemed, in my boyish ignorance, that in our state, geologically, nothing big had happened. But Gingko Petrified Forest was an exception. Here logs had once lain in the mud at the bottom of a lake. Lava had filled the lake. Because the lake bottom was mud, the logs petrified rather than burned. Logs had turned to stone! An event worthy of dramaturgy.

In the late Miocene, about seventeen million years ago, in what is now eastern Washington and northeastern Oregon, rivers of lava began spewing out of the earth. The cause of this outpouring, the largest known in Earth's history, is uncertain. Most geologists believe it was due to a plume of hot magma forming a hotspot in the earth's crust, like the ones that exist today under Yellowstone and the island of Hawaii.[5] How the plume was created is subject to debate. Some believe the plume occurred when an asteroid or comet collided with the earth and

---

[5] The Yellowstone hotspot may actually be the hotspot that caused the Columbia Plateau lava flood, and also caused the lava floods across the Snake River Plain and is likely, most geologists believe, to unleash lava floods again.

cracked the planet's crust. Whatever the cause, the lava was basalt, not the silica-rich andesite and rhyolite that occurs in explosive stratovolcanoes like Mount Rainier and Mount St. Helens. It was basalt and it flowed with the consistency of molasses and it was the same basalt that erupts from shield volcanoes like Mauna Loa in Hawaii and (perhaps, in the indeterminate past) from Olympus Mons on Mars, and it covered most of eastern Washington and parts of Oregon and Idaho and flowed all the way to the Willamette Valley in western Oregon and into the Pacific Ocean. The biggest flows erupted off and on during the next three million years. Lesser flows continued for the next eight million years. The totality of flows buried the region to a depth of over a mile and was so heavy the earth's crust sagged and the entire Columbia Basin tipped southwestward toward what is now the Columbia River Gorge. The flows didn't erupt continuously. When they did, the result was high drama. Forests flamed. Miocene rhinoceroses were encased by lava. Smoke blackened the sky. The earth's climate cooled. Then the eruptions abated. Forests reseeded. The rhinoceroses returned. The earth warmed. Destruction. Renewal. Destruction again. There were no people to witness this. But do we know the cycle in our bones? As in the *Bhagavad Gita*, chapter 11, verse 32: *Time I am, the destroyer of worlds. . . .*

Volcanoes, Ash, and Further Speculation on Catastrophe

Susan and I are driving from Walla Walla, in southeastern Washington, to Grand Coulee Dam, in the north-central part of the state. We are crossing the Columbia Basin following US 395 from the Tri-cities and SR-17 to Moses Lake. The land is a cornucopia of wheat, barley, mint, alfalfa, potatoes, hops, spearmint, sweet cherries, concord grapes, wine grapes, pears, prunes, plums, corn, lentils, onions, apricots, peaches, canola, garbanzo beans, even blueberries. It's a cornucopia because of its volcanic soil and it's a cornucopia because of Columbia River irrigation. After Mount St. Helens erupted in 1981, large areas here were blanketed by volcanic ash. The crops for the next few years were unusually lush. For the fifty-seven people who died in the eruption, Mount St. Helens was catastrophe. For the farmers in eastern Washington it was windfall.

Do we have an intuitive appreciation of catastrophe? Unlike deep time, maybe we do. Maybe childhood conditions us to at least the potential for disaster. *Walk on the left. Look both ways. Never talk to strangers.* Perhaps each of us knows we face the ultimate catastrophe in our deaths. Perhaps in the cycle of birth, life, and death, repeated over and over again, catastrophe becomes ingrained in us. We learn to coexist with it, to adapt to it. Like the Japanese mounting their tsunami stones, we take steps to ameliorate its consequences, if not for ourselves, at least for our descendants.

The word *catastrophe* is Greek and it means an overturning or a ruin or a conclusion—or all of these together. Suddenness is implied. So is violence. But it also contains an element of creation. Cataclysm destroys, but yields something new. There are physicists who theorize that our universe was birthed from a seething, probabilistic void, perhaps the cradle of many universes, in a single, searing instant. We know this as the Big Bang.

From the perspective of the void the Big Bang was a catastrophe.

For us it was creation.

Still, even today, the concept of cataclysm in geology is uncomfortable. Our grandparents probably accepted the idea more readily than we—had they not heard it again and again from the pulpits of their churches and synagogues and in the sermons of their preachers and rabbis and priests? But beginning with their generation and certainly by our parent's generation, laymen and experts alike came to a more gradualist view—the planet evolved slowly, over time, and by processes we could observe in our own age: wind and water erosion, the slow uplift of mountains– and it was this view, called geographic gradualism or *uniformitarianism,* that prevailed into my own childhood. At the time uniformitarianism was seen as liberation; religion had stultified naturalists for thousands of years forcing them to explain what they saw in terms of a seven-day creation and the Noahic flood. The Bible was, after all, catastrophist. Finally, science, at least nineteenth-century science, became gradualist.

Yet by the 1950s and 1960s new ideas and evidence were coming into play that upset the orderliness of gradualism: comets and meteorites crashing into the planet, perhaps several times; massive biological extinctions; reversal of the earth's magnetic field; cracks in the earth's crust unleashing lava flows that blanketed thousands of square miles. What was evolving was a theory both gradualist and catastrophic, and if much of the time the planet did evolve slowly, sometimes dramatic events altered the course of geology on a scale that was difficult to accept or even comprehend.[6]

Susan and I cross Interstate 90 on the outskirts of Moses Lake. We bypass this agricultural and retirement town and head north toward Ephrata and Soap Lake. We cross a flat, rocky wasteland, populated by small herds of cattle and large fields of rocks. House-sized rocks. Haystack-shaped rocks. Rocks arrayed in ranks like soldiers. White rocks. Black rocks. Rust-red rocks. The rocks are *erratics*, a geology term that means "from elsewhere" without specifying how elsewhere came to be anywhere—a rock from Moses Lake, for example, carried by us to our condo in Seattle would be called an erratic. The Ephrata rocks are from all over, British Columbia and Idaho and Montana, and they were carried here in the outflows of the world's greatest floods.

Dry Falls, Grand Coulees, Channeled Scablands, and the Great Ice Age Floods

It's mid-morning on a cool, spring Sunday in Steamboat Rock State Park at Banks Lake in the Grand Coulee in eastern Washington, twenty miles north of Soap Lake. The park is one of the most popular in Washington State, beloved for its warm waters and for its dry summer heat. The lake is a reservoir and it feeds the three thousand miles of irrigation canals that are the Columbia Basin Project. In summer, the temperature daily cracks one hundred degrees. Today it's in the forties and we walk briskly to keep warm. Susan and I are following a path along the shore. Cottonwoods and poplars frame an expanse of lawn. The leaves are celadon green. The grass lime green. Canada geese waddle before us in pompous parade. The park claims the entirety of a peninsula: on a map, it looks like a ground squirrel standing on its hind feet and sniffing the air. Behind us, Steamboat Rock looms over the otherwise flat peninsula and towers six hundred feet above the lake. Gray sagebrush foots the massif. Yellow

---

6 The idea of catastrophe in geology is relevant even on a modest scale. Stephen Jay Gould, in his 1980 collection of essays, *The Panda's Thumb*, notes that the official pamphlet for Arches National Park states that the sandstone arches were created by erosion "a few grains at a time," while a few pages later the same pamphlet describes the sudden collapse of Skyline Arch in 1940, so that the arch "was suddenly twice its former size." "The arches," Gould went on to say, "form by sudden, intermittent collapse and toppling, not by imperceptible removal by sand. Yet gradualist orthodoxy is so entrenched that the authors of this pamphlet failed to note the inconsistency between their own factual account and the stated theory of their introduction."

balsamroot and golden parsnip and blue lupine liven the gray. To the south, toward Dry Falls and Sun Lakes, curtains of rain. On the other side of a mirroring lagoon, fluted cliffs rise above talus skirts to over a thousand feet. The cliffs run right and left in both directions as far as we can see and the summits are flat as a tabletop. The cliffs, primarily basalt, present a surprising palette: black, saffron, rust, fawn, dun, moss, sage. Behind Steamboat Rock, across a mile of lake, are similar cliffs. We're standing on the floor of the largest coulee of all the coulees in the Columbia Basin. The Grand Coulee.[7] What we see is the consequence of catastrophe.

About fifteen thousand years ago, toward the end of the last ice age, a torrent of water swept through here. The first torrent carved this coulee, and subsequent torrents expanded it. The water arrived suddenly and it arrived in great volume and, over a period of two thousand years, it arrived at least forty or fifty times and it was very, very deep. So deep that the tops of the coulee cliffs, a thousand feet above us, were cut into a plexus of channels, hanging valleys, and dry falls, and were scattered with abraded, stream-rolled boulders signifying the water not only filled the entire Grand Coulee but flowed in high volume and at high speed over the top of the coulee walls and into adjacent coulees and into the Columbia River north and west of here.

What must it have been like? The climate cooler. The great Cordillera Ice Sheet that covered a third of North America terminating only few miles north of here. The vegetation grassy steppe. The steppe breezy and inhabited by wooly mammoths and giant ground sloths and saber-tooth tigers. The first peoples may have just arrived. They would hear the flood before they saw it. The ground would begin to shake. The animals would begin to stampede. Flights of birds would darken the sky. A strong wind would begin to blow. Then they would see it. A brown wall, at this point a thousand feet high, coming toward them at sixty miles per hour, carrying mud and mammoth-sized rocks and chucks of ice in its tumult, sweeping everything before it, and running, running, running for perhaps two or three days running, until it slows, grows

---

7   The word *coulée* is from French-Canadian. It originates from the French-Canadian trappers who were the first Europeans to explore the area and it means *flow*, which is a more accurate description for what formed the coulees than anything the French-Canadian trappers could have imagined.

deeper, backs up, the waters ponded behind constrictions farther south. The water not only fills the Grand Coulee. It fills most of eastern Washington. Picture water pouring into a sandbox: the water cuts channels in the sand. The flood cut coulees and channels in the loess and volcanic topsoil and the erosion-prone basalt of eastern Washington; it spilled west carving a wider Columbia River and creating Moses Coulee; it cut south into the Quincy Basin where it broke through to the Columbia through Crater Coulee, Potholes Coulee, and Frenchman Springs Coulee; it flooded south from what is now the city of Spokane carving channels through the loess hills of the Cheney-Palouse, leaving behind Lind Coulee and Washtucna Coulee and the Channeled Scablands; it flooded the Snake River with so much water the Snake flowed backwards; it ponded behind Wallula Gap creating a vast temporary lake geologists call Lake Lewis; it jetted through the Wallula at speeds approaching eighty miles per hour, rising to a thousand feet deep in the gap; it hollowed out the Columbia River channel from a classic V-shaped riverbed into a U-shaped gorge; it cut off the base of the tributary streams and left them hanging as waterfalls; it flooded thousands of square miles of lowland along the river including the entire Willamette Valley in western Oregon, where it left icebergs laden with huge, semi-tractor-truck-sized boulders; it cut a trench from the mouth of the Columbia River far out into what was then a much lower Pacific Ocean (a trench still there, under what is now a much deeper Pacific).

What caused this catastrophe?

It was this: three hundred miles east, near what is today Missoula, Montana, a lobe of the Cordillera Ice Sheet blocked the Clark Fork River with a dam of ice. The water backed up into Montana's mountain valleys and formed an enormous lake: Glacial Lake Missoula. The lake was two thousand feet deep. It held as much water as Lake Ontario. The ice dam held the lake in place. But ice floats and, if the water gets deep enough, an ice dam will float too. It got deep enough. The ice lifted and the dam collapsed and the flood raged. Not once, but forty or fifty times, and each time the dam reformed, the lake backed up, the ice lifted, the dam failed and unleashed another flood.[8] Although I've

---

8 The evidence for the multiplicity of the flood comes from the strandlines, similar to those step-like lines on reservoir banks that record the high-water marks at various seasons. Based on this evidence, the later floods were lesser floods, probably due to the climate warming and the water necessary to lift a smaller, lighter ice dam less.

known of these ice age floods for some years now (though not as a boy), I didn't appreciate their magnitude until I saw the videos of the waves from the 2008 Indian Ocean and the 2011 Japanese tsunamis. The Lake Missoula flood waves were ten times taller than the tallest tsunami waves. They were taller than the Eiffel Tower, taller than the Empire State Building, ten times taller than Niagara Falls.[9]

Despite the magnitude of these floods, despite the scars of their aftermath, despite the breadth of geography affected, for years the floods went unrecognized.

To love geology is to love puzzles. To do geology well is to do it afoot and afield. The geologic detective work to discover the floods is itself an endearing tale. An irascible scientist—quixotic in his personal life, fond of students, disdainful of superiors, dismissive of colleagues, attentive to detail, committed to field work, intuitive about clues, articulate in presenting his case both in his writings and in his speech—places his findings before his contemporaries who for three decades denigrate and disdain and deny them only to ultimately vindicate him and honor him. J Harlen Bretz loved puzzles and J Harlen Bretz loved the field and J Harlen Bretz was a Hollywood version of what a geologist should be.[10] He saw the potholes, plunge pools, dry falls, and ripple marks of the eastern Washington scablands for what they were: clues to the flood, clues that Bretz's chair-bound colleagues refused to see. It's a great story. But not the story that most interests me.

The story that interests me is the story of the people who lived on the edge of catastrophe. And this story raises several questions.

The first question is this: how did the first people deal with repeating, incomprehensible catastrophe? A catastrophe almost certainly witnessed by some of their number. A catastrophe that, over two millennia, occurred perhaps twice every century so that in every generation a few of these people would have

---

9 The Dry Falls in Grand Coulee were, during the flood, four times higher than Niagara Falls and flowed with a flow equivalent to the combined flow of all the rivers of the world.

10 Once arrested for shooting a neighbor's trespassing cat, given to bearding his colleagues like a relapsed sinner at a Sunday School picnic, known to lock his students in his basement until they deciphered his wine-cellar key, Bretz was irascible, flamboyant, and given to dramatic gesture. Ultimately he received his due. In 1965, The International Association for Quaternary Research held their annual meeting in the United States during which field trips were organized to the Columbia Plateau. Bretz received a congratulatory telegram from the meeting attendees that concluded, "We are all now catastrophists."

seen and survived a flood. How did they explain it? What did they do about it? What precautions, if any, did they take?

The second question is this: are today's scientists, engineers, industrialists, politicians, generals, geologists, actuaries, spymasters, environmentalists, oilmen, philosophers, artists, priests, rabbis, and imams any more apt in addressing catastrophes than the native peoples who were trying to deal with and explain the ice age floods?

My last question is this: did we need catastrophe to become the thinking creatures we are? There's a theory that at the end of the last ice age, when the climate and flora and fauna were radically changing, when many of the large predators and big-game animals were going extinct, one reason human beings survived and other carnivores didn't is because we had brains adapted to rapid change, perhaps even evolved by rapid change to the brains we now have.

Susan and I stand in the rain, looking at the clues in Grand Coulee: mazes, buttes, potholes, plunge pools, dry falls, cataract cliffs, strandlines, ripple marks, gravel bars a thousand feet above and miles distant from any running river. We try to imagine the flood. What would we have done? What is the meaning of this? What thing is the next thing that will be like ice age floods?

After we leave Grand Coulee, we follow US 2 west, dropping down into the adjacent Moses Coulee, climbing up over the mesa between Moses Coulee and the Columbia River. Rolling hills, by turn spring green and furrowed chocolate. The snow-whitened Cascade Mountains to the west. Silver light streaming through black clouds trailing gray gales of rain. As the highway rises, falls, and winds its way through the hills, Susan says, "Ripple marks?"

"Maybe," I answer, although I'm not certain.

But maybe Susan sees what Bretz saw: the footprints and fingerprints of the floods.

Grand Coulee Dam

It's one of the largest concrete structures in the world. It generates almost seven thousand megawatts of electricity. It's the fourth largest hydropower producer in the world. It's over five hundred feet high. It's over five thousand feet wide. It forms a reservoir one hundred fifty miles long with six hundred miles of shoreline. But statistics don't tell its tale. You have to see it. And once you've seen Grand Coulee Dam you won't forget Grand Coulee Dam.

Susan and I have checked into the Grand Coulee Inn. The inn clings to the side of a U-shaped canyon. Our room is tiny: a double bed, a small refrigerator, a TV, a stuffed chair with sagging springs, wood paneling; it's also spanking clean and it's sweet with the fragrance of the wood. I was here once before, twelve years ago, with two friends, both beautiful women, and our combined litter of five kids, three Chevy SUVs, and two boats on boat trailers. I remember the trip with affection. The hotel clerk greeted me by saying, "So you're the one with the two women." I felt like an Old Testament patriarch. Later, after we left the motel, after we set up camp on the Lake Roosevelt shore, after a night swept by lightning, thunder, and heavy rain, after waking to forty-degree temperatures, we drank martinis at ten o'clock in the morning to ward off the chill, to warm our bellies, and to thaw our souls. That afternoon, when our spouses arrived from Seattle, the weather was warmer and so were we.

The door of our room faces a steep hill behind the motel. The hill is planted with a stand of old tamarack trees, the trees just beginning to leaf, some with bird houses nailed to their trunks; the bird houses red, yellow, and blue. From our balcony we can hear mourning doves *coo, coo, cooing* their sweet, sad refrain. We watch a bald eagle soar above the river. We watch the dam.

The dam is enormous. But it's enormity without scale. As tall as Seattle's Space Needle, as wide as four Queen Marys laid bow to stern, containing enough concrete to pave a four-foot-wide sidewalk, four inches deep, twice around the waist of the world. But because the canyon defile is so deep, because the rock walls are so steep, because there are no houses or trees adjacent to the dam, because each of the three powerhouses are as long as at least several football fields (the largest and newest powerhouse, Powerhouse Three, seven football fields long), there's no perspective: we might be viewing a hydropower diorama.

A cat's cradle of high-tension cables loops down from the canyon walls to each of the three powerhouses. The spillway is the leitmotif for the dam: a five-hundred-foot high, half-mile-wide, manmade waterfall. Midsummer it roars and froths and thunders. Now, in mid-May, it's dry and still, more like the Egyptian Pyramids than a dynamic hydro plant, the only hint of its power the upwelling of the river at the base of each powerhouse. The level of Lake

Roosevelt behind the dam is seventy feet below the spillway gates, well below normal, deliberately lower in anticipation of a big runoff, the aftermath of a snowy winter and a cooler-than-normal spring. The causeway over the spillway spans a series of arches. The arches remind me of the arches on the Pont du Gard, a Roman aqueduct Susan and I visited in Provence last fall on a chilly, mistral-breezy afternoon. I wonder if the similarity is coincidence. Dam and aqueduct. Monuments to their superpower civilizations.[11]

During our summer vacations my father would travel out of his way to see a dam, especially if it was a dam under construction, and in those days, in the 1950s and 1960s, on the Columbia River, many dams were under construction. The three earliest, Rocky Reach, Grand Coulee, and Bonneville, had proved crucial to the World War II war effort, generating electricity for aluminum smelters, airplane factories, and shipyards, and for the then-top-secret Hanford facility, the place that produced the plutonium for the "Fat Boy" atomic bomb that America dropped on Nagasaki.

But if the war showed the national security import of hydropower, especially in the Pacific Northwest, it delayed the other purpose for which the dams were intended. Which was to make the desert bloom.

Back then I felt ambivalence toward deserts. Traveling in my parent's un-air-conditioned station wagon, the desert was a thirsty, sere, ennui-inducing wasteland, bereft of trees, populated by sagebrush and tumbleweeds, with an occasional jack rabbit or magpie to enliven its otherwise empty highways. Why not make it bloom? What we didn't see were the towns flooded, the native peoples displaced, the salmon genomes narrowed, the very geographical processes shaping the earth altered. Nor did we see what might happen should the dams fail. Back then Americans and Canadians loved dams and we were building them faster than we are ever likely to build them again. The Mica, the Revelstoke, the Keenleyside, the Grand Coulee, the Chief Joseph, the Wells, the Rocky Reach, the Rock Island, the Wanapum, the Priest Rapids, the McNary, the John Day, The Dalles, the Bonneville. And the dams we built evolved the Columbia no less than volcanism, glacial floods, and ice had evolved the Columbia.

---

11 The Pont du Gard is said to have delivered water to Nimes for hundreds of years after Rome fell, and may well have continued to be used as a toll bridge into the ninth century. We can hope that Grand Coulee Dam will be equally long lived.

Susan and I visit the Grand Coulee Visitor Center, a short walk from our motel. The visitor center is an upside-down Dixie Cup, supersized, cast in concrete. Below the center, above the river, is a wide, picnic-area lawn. Marmots—furry, squirrel-like creatures, fat as prairie dogs—graze across the grass. The Visitor Center is brightly lit and breezily informative. Exhibits address the conflicted genesis of the dam: the boosterism and rivalry between Wenatchee and Spokane, the argument of gravity irrigation versus pump irrigation, high dam versus low dam, Federal versus state versus private funding, irrigation versus electricity, the courts versus the Bureau of Reclamation versus Congress, the Great Depression and the New Deal, the engineering disasters and their concomitant resolutions. We listen to anecdotes recorded by dam workers, try out tools they used to build the dam, read expositions of how hydropower works, view art that commemorates the dam. You can push a button and hear Woodie Guthrie sing. "Roll on, Columbia. You can ramble to the sea, but river while you're rambling, you can do some work for me."[12]

Guthrie may have sung about the Columbia but it was the powder monkeys, bellboys, sand blasters, crane operators, hard-hat divers, engineers, cooks, welders, and journeyman laborers who dammed it. I have a great affection for these men, for their hard labor, for their skill, for the cooperative enterprise, a remnant of my parent's faith (and mine too) in the New Deal. Over five thousand men were employed in the construction of the dam. When work slowed, when materials ran short (once, the project ran out of cement and there wasn't enough cement in the entire United States of America to proceed), the workers were laid off. Does this knowledge diminish my affection for the enterprise? I decide not.

We tour the Third Powerhouse. Our group is small: two young couples, one couple with a toddler, Susan and I. No handbags or backpacks. We're required to pass through a metal detector. We board a van. An armed guard stands by. The couple with the toddler struggle to weave a child car seat into

---

12 Guthrie was on the Works Progress Administration payroll. He received $266.66 for this and other songs glorifying the enterprise. One historian suggests that the dam owes its existence to Guthrie's song, which generated public enthusiasm and support for the dam, as much as it does to Franklin Roosevelt, Congress, and the New Deal. Eleanor Roosevelt was less sanguine about the dam; on visiting the construction site with the president she is said to have quipped, "it was a good salesman who sold Franklin this dam."

the van seatbelt. "A Federal regulation," our guide says. He's a big, bald, bulky man in his late sixties, and he wears a battery-powered microphone-speaker pack strapped to his belt. He is also our driver. The van takes us down to the base of the dam. Armed guards patrol the gate to the dam and greet our van—the authorities are worried about terrorists. "The powerhouse," the guide informs us, "uses the same buttressed architecture as a medieval cathedral." Sure enough. Along the side of the white concrete exterior, we see a series of vertical, graceful, buttress-like bulges. The exterior is severe but attractive, the concrete patterned in an airy imprint like fossil leaves, the buttresses marching one after another the length of the building

But inside . . . inside, the Third Powerhouse *is* a cathedral; long like a cathedral (seven football fields long!), narrow like a cathedral, high-ceilinged like a cathedral, the light cool and indirect and softly green like in a cathedral. An enormous yellow rail crane arches over us, mounted on railroad tracks that run the length of the powerhouse. "Designed," our guide says, "to lift any of the six hydro generators completely free of its housing." A second, slightly smaller crane attaches to the ceiling. "For the generator exciters," the guide says. The cranes arch over us like vaults in a cathedral. The floor gleams. Six rings, each tiled blue, each flush with the floor, each the diameter of the length of a Greyhound bus, each circled by a waist-high rail, mark the tops of the hydro generators. The space is thrumming: a hollow sound like monks chanting. We descend to the next floor and view a generator rotor through glass windows. It spins majestically. Its speed at the rotor circumference is one hundred fifty miles per hour. It doesn't look that fast and it's not that fast, given the electricity generated, which is why the rotor and the stator are so large.[13] Below us, water from the reservoir courses through penstocks, great tunnels as wide as two school buses, then enters a scroll case, which is a sort of volute focusing the

---

13 The physics behind electrical generators have always daunted me, a complicated interaction of electrons, magnetic fields, and physical motion, acting at apparent cross-purpose. The "cross-purpose" part is explained to young engineering students by what is called the right-hand rule, where the directions of the current, magnetic field, and physical motion in a motor or a generator act in three dimensions and at right angles to one another, and may be represented by one's right hand: forefinger and index finger ninety degrees to each other while the thumb is vertical. During electrical-engineering exams at the Naval Academy when I was a midshipman, if you or the midshipman beside you was staring at your right hand with a puzzled expression, it portended ill for your exam grade.

stream, after which it passes through wicket gates, which are like throttles that open and close as the river flow or electricity demand varies, until the water finally impinges on the turbine blades, which spin, and which, in turn, spin the rotor, which has its own electrical field, and it's this field, rotating within the densely wired stator, that generates electricity in the wires of the stator. A lot of electricity. Eight hundred megawatts of electricity. Electricity that runs your air conditioner, your flat-panel TV, your computer, your Internet connection, your office copy machine, your hair dryer, your vanity lights, your cellphone relay towers, your bank cash machine, your supermarket cash registers, your stove and your heat and, someday, perhaps, even your car.

Our guide drives us up to the top of the dam, shows us the penstocks that transfer irrigation water up to Banks Lake, cites statistics about Lake Roosevelt and the National Recreation Area that encloses the lake. But nothing has moved me like the Third Powerhouse. Our era is called the Information Age, the Telecommunication Age, the Wired Age, the Internet Age, the Social Networking Age. None of these "ages" could exist without electricity. What we're in, it seems to me, is the Electrical Age, and the Third Powerhouse is one of its high cathedrals.

Susan and I breakfast at a café called Flo's. During the dam's construction, the neighborhood around Flo's was a twenty-four-hour red-light district. Bars, bawdiness, and brothels. "The cesspool of the New Deal," one journalist wrote. Now Flo's is more sedate. The kind of place where plaques on the wall say things like "Stomp your feet if you believe in Jesus" and "The Beatings Will Continue Until Morale Improves." The clientele is mostly local. Retirees in baseball caps, work boots, and jeans, the men and women dressed pretty much alike. There's been a rodeo in town; a few diners look like wranglers. A new couple enters. A guy and a woman. Thirty or so. The guy is wearing a sweatshirt. Blue with gold letters. US Naval Academy. The trireme crest. *Ex Temper Tridents.* "From knowledge, sea power."

"Go Navy," I call out.

"Beat Army," the guy responds. It's the Naval Academy call and response.

Our wives—Susan and the woman we'll soon learn is this guy's wife—both look embarrassed. It turns out that my fellow grad—"shipmates" is what we call ourselves—has just completed his XO tour on an Ohio-class Trident-missile submarine and is on his way to a new assignment in Norfolk, Virginia. Like me, he's nuclear-power trained, although I'm many years out of the navy and, unlike him, was a surface rather than submarine officer.

"I had to see the dam," he explains. "I guess because I'm a nuke."

I hear you brother.

For a few seconds, we share something, not just by being old grads and naval officers and nukes, but we share something about electricity, about the brotherhood and sisterhood of electricity, about membership in an order that has in this electric age been its priests and acolytes and evangelists, its deacons and choirmasters and collection-plate passers, its enablers. Without us, no electricity. And then, what would the future be?

The Atom, the Bomb, and Hanford Reach

We're driving, Susan and I, south from Vantage, in the middle of Washington State, where I-90 crosses the Columbia, through a wide, U-shaped valley carved by the ice age floods, the bluffs on both sides remnant of Miocene lava flows, their colonnades Columbia River basalt, black, columnar, fluted resembling castles and monasteries and battlements. "The sagebrush is actually purple," Susan says. She's right. In this late afternoon light, the sagebrush *is* purple and we're motoring through a Zane Grey novel, auto-borne *Riders of the Purple Sage*. The last time I traveled this way was fifty years ago, with my father, and the highway we followed then is now underwater. This stretch is a reservoir lake, Priest Rapids Lake, and it's dammed behind Priest Rapids Dam. The reservoir is not especially wide; it still looks like a river. The new highway follows a flat, tabletop ledge above the reservoir. We spot a gathering of people in cowboy hats, drinking beer amid a clutch of SUVs and pickup trucks and a half-dozen American flags billowing in a brisk breeze. Osama Bin Laden was killed this week—is this an impromptu celebration? As we proceed south, the sagebrush gives way to orchards white with blossoms. Are they apples or peaches or pears? We pass a golf course and a retirement community. *Desert Aire.* It's a marvelous, magical, dreamlike drive, unexpected, unforgettable, what I love about car travel, what you never get when you travel by air.

We cross the river downstream of the Priest Rapids Dam. Briefly, we enter

Hanford Reach National Monument, exit it, and skirt its west-bank segment for the next thirty miles.[14] The monument includes portions of the east bank of the river, as well as the mountains to the west. Saddle Mountain and Rattlesnake Mountain. There has been no farming here since 1943. No dams, ever. It is the last free-flowing section of the Columbia River in eastern Washington, the only non-tidal, free-flowing section in the United States. It has oxbow bends, ponds, river sloughs, gravel bars, riffles, and fluvial islands. It's a spawning ground for salmon and steelhead. The monument's desert plateaus and rugged hills are habitat for rare desert elk, for forty-two mammal species, two hundred fifty bird species, four amphibian species, eleven reptile species, and fifteen hundred invertebrate species, a number of which are threatened or endangered or have vanished elsewhere from the Columbia Plateau.

And the monument is a paradox.

The paradox is this: it owes its preservation to the greatest threat (so far) to our own species: The Atomic Bomb. The Hanford Reach National Monument was once the security buffer for the Hanford Nuclear Reservation, and Hanford is where America refined the plutonium for the first atomic explosive device (the Alamogordo bomb), and for the second (the "Fat Boy" bomb that incinerated forty-five thousand Japanese souls in Nagasaki and that ended World War II—and the last bomb ever used in actual warfare), and the plutonium employed in the American Armageddon arsenal built to win the Cold War (which, perhaps, *did* win the Cold War, or at least played an important part in winning it, and that wasn't, thankfully, ever used in a hot war).[15] It is also the most polluted place in America.

The siting of an atomic facility at Hanford offers several lessons in technological blindness, willful and otherwise. The decision to build Hanford was made hastily and it was made in secrecy, understandable given the suspicion that Nazi Germany was building a similar weapon. The main concerns in choosing the site were remoteness from population, military defensibility, the availability of lots of electricity and lots of cold water. Geological stability was

---

14 A "monument" in this sense, is not a statue, but a park in the National Park system created by presidential proclamation rather than by an act of Congress.
15 It was the Alamogordo bomb, also known as the Trinity Bomb, that occasioned Robert Oppenheimer, the project's lead scientist, to experience, on witnessing the bomb's detonation, his famous theophany. "Now I am become Death, the destroyer of worlds."

desirable, but, given the haste and the secrecy, a thorough analysis couldn't be done. Had it been done, the area might still have been declared "stable." Much was still unknown: Bretz's ice age floods had not yet become geological rote, the nearby Cascade volcanoes, including Mount St. Helens, were considered "dormant," and the proximity of the several tectonic plates (and tectonics in general) was completely unknown. What's more, General Leslie Groves, the head of the Manhattan Project charged with building the bomb, had already decided that somewhere in the Northwest was the ideal location. "If because of some unknown and unanticipated factor a reactor were to explode and throw great quantities of highly radioactive materials into the atmosphere when the wind was blowing toward Knoxville [a site in Tennessee that was an alternative to Hanford]," Groves wrote in his memoirs, "the loss of life and damage to health in the area might be catastrophic."[16] Early on, the scientists and engineers on the project recognized that there would be large quantities of radioactive waste, much of it liquid. The reason for this is because of the way plutonium 239, a highly fissile isotope that can be used to build an atomic bomb, is produced. Plutonium 239 doesn't occur naturally. To get it, you radiate uranium 238 in a reactor. Then you separate the plutonium from a lot of other unpleasantly radioactive stuff and you do this by grinding everything up and bathing it in acid. Needless to say, you get a lot of liquid waste. The geology of the Hanford area, also known as the Pasco Basin, was seen as ideal: a deep, mostly gravel-till formation that was a good retention medium for liquids and that would hold the liquid in place. What the geologists didn't understand was that the gravel was gravel laid down as a giant gravel bar by the ice age floods, the Bretz floods, and that underneath the gravel was another layer of compressed river bottom sediments known as the Ringold Formation, formerly the bed of the ancestral Columbia River, and that this formation did transport waste, and that the direction of transport was toward the Columbia.[17] Other egregious radioactive

---

16 In General Groves defense, neither he nor the civilian contractors employed at Hanford, imagined the nuclear reservation lasting beyond the end of World War II. Because of the Cold War, it lasted nearly four decades, and ended up at its peak production refining enough plutonium every two days to build the equivalent of one Nagasaki bomb.

17 "Like roads to Rome," wrote geologist J Harlen Bretz in 1959 describing why the flows that deposited the gravels were where they were, "all scabland rivers led to the Pasco Basin."

discharges occurred at Hanford. More than 684,000 curies of radioactivity were discharged directly into the river. By way of comparison, the Three Mile Island nuclear meltdown in Pennsylvania in 1979 discharged fifteen curies. Traces of Hanford radioactivity were measured as far south as the California coast and as far north as British Columbia.[18] But the groundwater pollution may be the most serious problem, because it may be the problem almost impossible to clean up, and the contaminated water may be migrating toward the river and could become, over a number of years, a chronic source of radioactive pollution in the Columbia. Over four hundred forty billion gallons of hazardous liquids, not all radioactive, were dumped into the ground at Hanford.

Another paradox of Hanford Reach is that here was where the public said "No more Columbia dams." The opinion wasn't unanimous. One Washington senator, Senator Slade Gordon, supported a Hanford Reach dam. The other senator, Senator Patty Murray, opposed it. I love Murray's testimony. "We have asked much of the Columbia River," she testified, "and it has always given generously. It has given us affordable energy, turned a desert into a farming oasis, and provided a highway for international commerce. Shouldn't we allow it to keep its one last wild Chinook [salmon] run?"

Redfish Lake and What do we do about the Salmon?

With our dear friends, Tom and Jody Beckwith, Susan and I own a house in Idaho's Big Wood River Valley. The valley is the site of the Sun Valley Ski Resort and it's the location of the town of Ketchum and the town is famous, at least in literary circles, as the mountain retreat of Ernest Hemingway and the place where Hemingway took his own life. The Big Wood is also part of the Columbia River watershed, and the Big Wood finds its way to the Snake River and the Snake River finds its way to the Columbia. The mountains in the area—the Smokies, the Boulders, the Pioneers, the Sawtooths, and the White Clouds—form a western buttress to the Rocky Mountains and count among their number Idaho's highest peaks. North of Ketchum is Galena Pass and

---

18 Because we live on a radioactive planet, because we measure radioactivity against background radiation, because we assume background is constant, which it's not, scientists assumed the curies dumped into the river would be diluted and become undetectable, as though they never existed, as if we'd wished them away.

on the other side of the pass is a lovely sagebrush valley between the White Cloud and Sawtooth ranges. The valley is the headwaters of the Salmon River, also known by its more romantic moniker, The River of No Return, and, at the valley's northern end, is Redfish Lake, nestled below Mount Hyndman, a ten-thousand-footer, and the Grand Mogul, a nine-thousand-footer. The lake was once a cirque of a Sawtooth Range glacier. Its elevation, at over six thousand feet, is so high that when we launch our Boston Whaler runabout here, we have to install a special propeller to compensate for lack of oxygen to power the boat's outboard engine. We love this lake. We've spent many afternoons here, swimming, waterskiing, hiking, playing on its sandy pocket beaches.

The lake and the river derive their names from the sockeye salmon that once spawned here in such numbers the lake turned red with their presence. The sockeye are *anadromous*. They are born in freshwater, migrate to the sea, and return to their natal stream or lake. They are also *semelparous*, meaning they spawn once and die. A few sockeye still make it to Redfish. To get here, they have crossed the Columbia River bar from the Pacific Ocean, navigated three dams and three fish ladders, entered the Snake, ascended more dams and more fish ladders, navigated Hells Canyon (the deepest canyon in North America), ascended the Salmon, breasted rapids, avoided raptors, raccoons, and bears, climbed six thousand feet in elevation, and traveled a thousand miles. This is, of course, only half their lifetime journey. The first half, from the lake to the sea as smolt, was even more perilous.

Recently I viewed a PBS *Nature* documentary, called "Salmon: Running the Gauntlet." The program addressed the salmon in the Columbia River Watershed, specifically the sockeye salmon, and how the sockeye are under severe stress, and how the steps people have taken to preserve the runs—hatcheries, fish ladders, artificial breeding—are failing. The sockeye salmon, at least in the Columbia River Watershed, face catastrophe.

The video is beautiful. The perils of the salmon are graphically and movingly presented. There are a number of interviews: scientists, hatchery managers, activists, Native Americans, historians. The speakers are urgent, articulate, predicative, pessimistic. One interview particularly caught my attention. The interviewee was a man in his sixties, my age, whose family had had a cabin on the Salmon River near Redfish Lake. The man's grandfather had lain awake at night, unable to sleep, for the noise of the sockeye returning to the lake. In his life, the man said, he hadn't even seen *one* salmon. Were they still there?

I love salmon and I love Redfish Lake and I love the Salmon River and the Snake River and Hells Canyon and the Columbia, and I have spent some of the best hours of my life camping, hiking, boating, river-rafting, and waterskiing in these waters. Yet, I found myself pausing at the man's statement. This man was describing salmon runs that took place in his grandfather's lifetime. What world did his grandfather live in? Did his Idaho neighbors have electricity? Was it a world inhabited by far, far fewer people? Was it a world where polio crippled and typhoid killed? Where many, many mothers died in childbirth? Where black women had to ride at the back of buses? Where their husbands and brothers and sons could be lynched without retribution? Where antisemitism and white racism were acceptable? Where women couldn't vote? Where nobody gave a damn if mines polluted, factories spewed waste, forests were clear cut, farms engendered dustbowls?

Was his world our world?

No. It wasn't.

So, you say, what does that matter? The sockeye are still dying. Why not turn back the clock? Why not get rid of the dams?

My answer is this: to save the sockeye we must work out a twenty-first-century solution, not a nineteenth-century solution. If in some ways this man's grandfather's world may have been better than ours; in more ways, it wasn't, and the things that make our world superior are the result of our technologies: more food, better food, fewer hungry people, fewer sick people, longer lives, brighter light, warmer homes, more homes, more schools, better schools, more universities and more students able to attend universities, more tolerance, more diversity, more information and (if you take the time to look for it and to vet it) better information. And, like it or not, our world is a new world. To paraphrase a much-paraphrased phrase, environmentally speaking, *We're not in Kansas anymore.*

To save the sockeye requires the hard, unglamorous business of forging coalitions, negotiating compromises, forgoing the false promise of back-to-Eden idealism.[19] It requires a redefinition of stewardship. One not solely about the environment but not solely about civilization either. Can we strike a balance? Some deserts made to bloom? Others left alone? Some rivers dammed? Others left to run free?

Houseboat

I want to end on a memory, an evening fourteen years ago. It's 1997. We are with our dear friends the Beckwiths, Tom and Jody, and their sons, Mac and Connor. Susan is there; so is our son John, and the boys are six, seven, and eight years old and we are on a Lake Roosevelt rental houseboat, an ungainly craft, more like an RV on pontoons than a boat. It's July and it's a warm night and the air is dry and the boys are still swimming and they are climbing to the top of the houseboat deck and they are jumping from the deck into the lake and then climbing back aboard and jumping again, and it's late, it's ten 'o'clock, and the moon is full and we don't have the heart to ask the boys to quit and we are into our third bottle of wine anyway and the houseboat is beached on the sand in a tiny cove beneath a desert cliff and the lake is so still the track of the moon on the water is like a highway to the stars and the air smells of pine and we are playing Chris Botti CDs on the houseboat stereo—have you heard Botti, one of the sweetest jazz trumpeters in the world?—and the four of us are on the top deck, good friends, sitting and watching the moon and listening to the music and the laughter of our boys and reminiscing and savoring this place, this moment, this lake, this night, our boys, each other, a moment so close to perfect, so far from the cataclysms and travails of the world, as close to perfection as any mortal could desire, so perfect we want it to last forever.

Oh, Columbia. Roll on, roll on.

---

19   Some years ago our family and friends rafted down the Salmon River. On our last night we camped at the juncture of the Salmon and the Snake Rivers. It was a great amphitheater, a sandy, stepped beach, below brick-red cliffs, at the bottom of Hells Canyon. The next day we'd raft the Snake. "Jet boats," we complained. "There goes the peace and quiet." But our trip leader rebuked us. "Jet-boaters love the river too," he said. "It's the alliance of all those who love it that will save it."

Volcano: An A to Z

We have been poor at assimilating the great lessons that geology teaches—the earth's ceaseless motion and immensity of time . . . I well remember the catechism I learned in grade school: Mt. Lassen, which erupted in 1914, is the only active volcano in the United States (Alaska and Hawaii were still colonial possessions at the time).
—Stephen Jay Gould, "Deep Time and Ceaseless Motion," *The New York Review of Books,* May 14, 1981

A. Attitude and Altitude

WE GREW UP UNDER A VOLCANO, my sister, my two brothers, my schoolmates, my future wife, Susan, and I. Massive, silent, snow-covered, ice-capped, at fourteen thousand feet it presided over us, although we rarely thought of it as a volcano. We saw it more like one of those great-uncles: distant, benign, reassuring by his constancy, evidence of something larger than immediate family. The Salish, who lived under it, called it Tahoma. Captain George Vancouver, the first European to officially see it, named it Rainier. We natives called it "The Mountain." Nowadays three million of us live in its shadow. Even when we can't see it—and in misty Pacific Northwest winters we often can't—we're cognizant of its presence. Maybe because its likeness is everywhere: on license plates, beer bottles, business logos, and at least two baseball teams. Maybe because it has become our trademark, the leitmotif for regional identity. Maybe because, at its fourteen-thousand-foot altitude, it's impossible to ignore. We live in its shadow, and we're mostly happy to live there. But it's a Damoclean shadow: the United States Coast and Geodetic Service has designated Rainier the most hazardous volcano in the lower forty-eight states. In the last thousand years, on sixty different occasions, Rainier rained destruction on Puget Sound: eruptions, earthquakes, ash, pyroclastic flows, mud, debris-laden lahars.

We grew up under a volcano not thinking it a volcano.

But it was.

And it still is.

B. Burroughs Mountain

Every other September or so I put on my hiking boots and pack my daypack and drive up to Mount Rainier National Park's White River entrance. There I ascend the highway to Yakima Park. Next to the Rainier National Park Company's one-time lodge, now a caféteria and gift shop, I begin the trail to Burroughs Mountain. I like this trail because of its open views and because you begin in flowered meadows but eventually climb well above the tree line and because it is a loop and you don't have to retrace your steps. I prefer a counter-clockwise route that gets you higher faster, but also I like the drama of it. You don't see the mountain until you complete the ascent up First Burroughs, and then, upon reaching a wide, flat, treeless plateau that tops the Burroughs sum-mit (formed when a lava flow filled in a canyon), the mountain reveals itself: to the west Winthrop Glacier, to the east the chimney spire of Little Tahoma, dead ahead Camp Sherman, and above Sherman, Steamboat Prow at 9,600 feet, and above Steamboat Prow, the massive fourteen-thousand-foot Liberty Cap, white as a sailor's hat. The soil on First Burroughs is gray and crumbly: it's frozen most of the year. Only a few hardy wildflowers and heather can survive here, but there are marmots (relatives of ground hogs) and golden-mantled ground squirrels (which look like chipmunks) and hawks that ride the after-noon thermals. Sometimes a mountain goat steps tentatively out of the fog.

C. Composite Volcanoes

Mount Rainier, like most other Cascade Range volcanoes, is a composite or stratovolcano made up of discontinuous layers of lava, ash, and tephra, tephra being clast (rock larger in size than ash) that has been hurled into the sky and fallen back to the earth. Because this mixture of lava, ash, and tephra doesn't flow readily, composite volcanoes are usually steep-sided. The characteristic profile of a composite volcano is conical: think Fuji in Japan or Popocatépetl in Mexico or, before it blew its top, St. Helens in Washington State. Because their strata are of different materials, composite volcanoes are not only subject to explosive eruptions—magma rising, pressure building, domes exploding in a hail of material that can rise twelve miles into the atmosphere—but also to landslides and mudflows that can be triggered with or without seismic activity. The lava rock, weakened by geothermal chemistry, and the layers of frangible ash and loose tephra, augmented by ice and snow and mud, combine in a concrete-like slurry called a *lahar* that will speed down the mountain at up to forty miles per hour and up to distances of more than fifty miles. Near the volcano, lahars flatten houses, knock down three-hundred-foot trees, rip boulders from the ground. Farther downstream they entomb everything. Lahars are the leading cause of volcanic death. And the toll is grim. Tambora in Indonesia killed 92,000. Krakatau also in Indonesia 36,000. Mount Pelée in Martinique 30,000. Nevada del Ruiz in Columbia 25,000. And these are only the big ones, the famous ones, the recent ones. Since the beginning of recorded history, killer volcanoes have snuffed out more than 300,000 human lives. Today, at the dawn of the twenty-first century, over 150,000 Puget Sounders live in the path of Rainier's historical lahars.

D. Death

What is the calculus of death?

Not too many weeks ago, my father-in-law Dick Cole died. More than a hundred people attended his memorial service. After the service, we gathered at our house—there were so many of us you could hardly walk from room to room until eventually we spilled out the front door and onto our front porch and into the cool March afternoon. We honored Dick. We celebrated his life. And the ritual comforted us.

Each evening the PBS *News Hour* broadcasts photographs of the soldiers, sailors, and marines who have died in the previous days' battles in Afghanistan and Iraq. I always stop what I'm doing and stand in silence until the last photograph flickers across the screen. I love these men and women. I love them for their ultimate sacrifice. I love them even though they are strangers to me and even though I doubt we have much common. I hope I never forget them.

Often, however, it seems to me that their honor guards and their rifle salutes and their half-masted banners and their photos and my silences aren't enough. They remain strangers, their names too easily forgotten.

After the 9/11 attacks, *The New York Times* printed a photograph and a brief memoriam for every one of the 2,998 victims. I see this as very American, this recognizing of each individual, and I believe it to be one of the best attributes of our national character. But in the 2007 Indian Ocean Earthquake, in a matter of hours, a tsunami swept a quarter of a million people to their deaths, possibly the most people killed in a single day's event in all of human history. So where were the silences and rifle salutes and half-masted banners for these sons and daughters? Who recited their names? How is it that so few of us bother to remember them? Are we predisposed to distance ourselves from a stranger's death? Do we have some built-in protection against too much death?

E. Enumclaw

Enumclaw lies at the base of the Cascade foothills, a ten-thousand-person community, forty miles southeast of Seattle and forty miles northwest of Mount Rainier. It's midway between the volcano's summit and the Space Needle. It was once a logging town. It's still a dairy town. Now it's evolving into a commuter town supporting the megalopolis growing out from Seattle and Tacoma. If it's a clear day when you drive around Enumclaw, you'll stumble upon vistas of the mountain, startling by its size and its white grandeur. But mostly the town-site is flat. Here and there, amid dairies and horse farms, hemlock-and-Douglas-fir-covered hills rise up as if they were islands rising in a meadow sea. In a sense, the hills are islands: glacial drumlins and scarps that stood above the river of mud that, 5,700 years ago, flowed down from the summit of Rainer. During that event, the mud in Enumclaw was at least seventy-five feet deep. The mud is why Enumclaw is flat. The event is known as the Osceola Mudflow. It's the largest such event in Rainier's history. One of the largest mudflows in the history of the world. Geologists believe that the Osceola occurred when the top two thousand feet of Rainier's summit collapsed, probably but not certainly from a volcanic eruption, but possibly from an earthquake in combination with the weakening of the summit by hydrothermal chemistry—magma heating groundwater, making it hot and acidic, converting hard volcanic rock into soft, clay-rich soil. In the high, glacial valleys nearer the summit, the mud depth exceeded three hundred feet. Imagine it. Mud hundreds of feet high. Mud floating house-sized chunks of summit breccias. Mud that would ultimately ground the breccias on scarps here in Enumclaw like icebergs in a mud sea. Mud rising as high as the tallest trees. Mud flowing faster than you could walk or run. Nobody knows how fast the mud actually flowed—was it fifteen or twenty or forty miles per hour? Could you hear it coming? Would it have sounded like waves breaking on a beach, like a hurricane of mud, like a freight train of mud? Mud that if you lived in Enumclaw then, and some Native Americans did, would entomb your lodge in less than forty minutes.

F. Fuji

Of the thirty-six woodblock prints by the Japanese artist Katsushika Hokusai, who lived from 1760 to 1849, the most famous is *The Great Wave off Kanagawa*. In this print a wave extends its tendrils over two slender boats just rising up from a trough. But the boats don't center the print. What centers the print is the small, perfect cone of Mount Fuji, which Hokusai placed at the bottom of the trough. What draws your attention is Fuji's solitude. Perhaps solitude is inherent in volcanoes. Like us, they are individuals. They stand apart from sister mountains. Perhaps this is why we identify volcanoes with our own solitary existences. My favorite Hokusai is *Mount Fuji in Clear Weather*, also known as *Red Fuji*. In this print Fuji is larger, its lower slope rising from the bottom left to its summit at the top right. The dominant colors are rose, green-blue, blue-black, and white: the base of the mountain is green-blue; the sky is a darker blue scalloped by white clouds; the top of the mountain is blue-black and streaked with white snow. But it's the middle of the mountain that draws your attention: the middle is rose, illuminated by an off-print sun rising. I love it because it reminds me of Rainier. The rising sun. The rare, rosy dawns. What I call Rainier's maraschino mornings.

G. Graveyard

Rainier is a graveyard.

My friend, Jay Ulin, who was once a climbing guide on Mount Rainier recently invited me to an ash-spreading in honor of Jay's friend and well-known climber Dick McGowan. The ceremony was held at Camp Muir, which is at the ten-thousand-foot level on the mountain and which is the kick-off point for climbers' final summit assault. Then those able would carry Dick's remains on his final climb so as to spread Dick's ashes on the summit. The mourners drove up to Paradise Inn, at six thousand feet. From there they climbed to Muir. I didn't join them—I didn't know Dick– but someday I'd like to hike up to Muir with Jay. I'd like to hear his tales of 1960s mountaineering, his accounts of his forty-four summit climbs. I've seen no statistics but I suspect there must be a number of ash-spreadings on Rainier—if you're a Puget Sounder, especially if you're a climber, the mountain is a holy place. But Rainier is a graveyard in other ways. Over five hundred people have lost their lives on its slopes: climbers, skiers, hikers, snowboarders, aviators. The National Park Service projects that each year two more people will die. The worst single incident occurred in 1946 when a US Navy transport carrying Marines from San Diego to Seattle, in bad weather and with no visibility, flew into the South Tahoma Glacier. The thirty-two men are still on the mountain, entombed in South Tahoma's ice.

The writer William Vollmann begins his essay "Three Meditations on Death" with the sentence, *Death is ordinary.* I suppose it is. But the only dead person I ever saw dead was my father, who died in his bed at the age of eighty-three. I don't recall feeling ordinary about that. Of course Vollmann's point is that death is so common it *should* feel ordinary.

Most climbers die in rockfalls or avalanches or just falling—down a snow-field, off a cliff, into a crevasse. Often they die in inclement weather, when the risks of avalanche, exposure, or just not being able to see where they are going are greatest.

But when I look at Rainier, I don't think death.

And that, it seems to me, is one of its paradoxes.

H. Haiku

I'm not a student of haiku. But I like the form, its Zen-like puzzle, its illusory simplicity, its ability to illuminate what lies between thought and words. The Mount Fuji volcano has inspired countless Japanese haiku artists. One of the most beloved Japanese haiku masters, Matsuo Basho (1644–1694), penned several about Fuji during his lifetime. Here are two:

> *clouds for roots,*
> *Mount Fuji's green foliage,*
> *the shape of a cedar*

> *over one ridge*
> *do I see winter rain clouds?*
> *snow for Mount Fuji*

I. Ice

There is more ice and snow on Mount Rainier than on all the other Cascade volcanoes combined. It is the most glaciated US peak outside of Alaska and hosts twenty-six different glaciers. If volcanism raised Rainier, ice sculpted it, gave it its rugged, cowboy-hero face, and ice is why it gleams so whitely over Puget Sound even on the hottest summer days.

Like Hokusai's *Thirty-Six Views of Fuji,* Rainier might be viewed from the perspective of each of its twenty-six glaciers. From the Nisqually, on the mountain's south side, the peak is almost conical; from the West Side Highway (now closed to automobiles), where the Kautz, Tahoma, and Puyallup glaciers descend, you see the craggy, vertical, wide-shouldered face of the Sunset Amphitheatre, which, as its name suggests, looks like an amphitheatre; in the northwest quadrant of the park, the Mowich, Edmonds, and Russell Glaciers border the precipitous and blasted scarp of Willis Wall; from the North, the Winthrop and Edmonds flow down either side of Steamboat Prow; from the east, my favorite glacier, the Frying Pan, skirts the chimney-like stack of Little

Tahoma, while from the southeast, the Cowlitz and Ingraham reach all the way to the summit where Columbia Crest leans west into the wind like a steam locomotive, Disappointment Clever its coal car, Little Tahoma its caboose. There is in the mountain's symbiosis of fire and ice something animate, something always on the edge of danger.

J. John Mathison

My father, John Mathison, attempted to climb Mount Rainier in 1952. He made it to within three hundred feet of the summit before his party had to turn back: one of the party (not my father) was suffering altitude sickness. I remember my father returning after the climb, bewhiskered, sunburned, his face still smeared with sunscreen, wearing his army-surplus climbing knickers, and carrying his army-surplus alpine backpack. He hadn't made it—but I felt no less proud of him than if he'd been an astronaut returning from the moon.

Hazard Stevens and Philemon Van Trump are generally credited as the first two people to climb Rainier. When they reached what they thought was the summit in August 1870 (now called Point Success) they subsequently saw a higher point (now called Columbia Crest). Because it was 5:00 p.m., because the climb had taken much longer than they expected, because they had to spend the night in the mountain's crater anyway, they opted to ascend the real summit the next morning. They had no tent and no warm clothing but they discovered a snow cave warmed by a sulfurous steam vent. "We passed a most miserable night," Stevens later wrote, "freezing on one side and in a hot steam-sulfur bath on the other."

The first woman to climb the mountain was Fay Fuller, daughter of a Tacoma, Washington, newspaper publisher. Ms. Fuller was twenty when she climbed Rainier in 1890 accompanied by four men and no other women, which scandalized Tacoma society, as did her climbing outfit of ankle-length wool bloomers, a jumper blouse, a full-skirted coat, goggles, a straw hat, and an alpenstock made of a shovel handle with a spike on the end.

Every year over eight thousand people attempt to climb Rainier: about half make it, the rest turning back mostly due to bad weather. My brother, Charles Mathison, a climber with a number of Cascade summits to his credit, summitted Rainier twice and on his third, failed attempt spent a night in a snow cave. My sister Charlotte Guyman and her husband Doug have also reached the summit, neither of them climbers; it seems to me their accomplishment is something else, more like running a marathon or cycling from Seattle to Portland, something you do to lengthen your list of accomplishments, something that does honor to you but less to the mountain. There's something in our culture that drives us to catalog accomplishments, to compete constantly (even when we're supposedly relaxing), to set aside too little time to savor what we experience. I liked the way the Mountaineers used to climb Rainier: beginning early in the spring they climbed the lesser Cascade peaks, Mount Si, Mount Pilchuck, graduating in early summer to St. Helens and Adams and sometimes Baker, culminating in July with the ascent of Rainier.

I have not climbed Rainier, which is not to say I wouldn't try, although at my age of sixty-one such an attempt would not be casually undertaken. But my not climbing the mountain hasn't made the mountain a lesser thing in my life.

The mountain is rooted in me.

And I in it.

K. Klapatche Park

The high meadows of Mount Rainier are called "parks." Klapatche Park was the first I ever reached by my own muscle and sweat. Back then, in 1960, the trail began on the West Side Highway, now closed to auto traffic, and it was short, only two and a half miles in length, but in that distance you ascended nearly two thousand feet. I was twelve years old when my dad and my ten-year-old brother, Charlie, and I set out on this hike. (The next winter I would write a one-paragraph essay about our ascent, which my seventh grade English teacher, Mr. Barr, would read aloud to the class, one of the first public performances of my writing.) The hike followed a pattern familiar to Rainier hikers: it began in a dense and dim conifer forest, where the ground had been softened by millennia of fallen needles and fallen trees and where the firs and hemlocks and cedars rose as high as two hundred feet. Then the trail began to climb in a series of switchbacks to where the ground grew stonier, the tree trunks, now Alaska yellow cedar and noble fir and white bark pine, more slender and the sunlight

brighter. Eventually, in a last steep pitch, the trail ascended into the first meadow, cupped below the mountain's skirt, dotted with tarns and stunted Engel-
mann spruce and noble fir and the brilliant herbaceous green of the meadow
grasses and sedges, which, if you looked more closely, were flowered with color:
red paintbrush, blue lupine, yellow avalanche lilies, cream-colored bear grass,
and purple asters. We lunched by a tarn that mirrored the mountain's face.
Insects droned a sleepy August fugue. Running water played a background
counterpoint. Resins from the trees and the fragrances of wildflowers perfumed
the air. Later we followed the trail up a talus slope to St. Andrews Lake, situat-
ed well above the tree line, where cairns marked the trail across stony fellfields.
In less than three miles we had passed through four life zones—Canadian,
Hudsonian, subalpine, and alpine—the equivalent at sea-level of walking from
Seattle to the Arctic Circle. Over the next few years my brother and I would
hike to many other parks: Van Trump, Indian Henry's, Summerland, Spray,
Berkley, Grand, Indian Bar—all would be wonderful. None would offer the
unique joy of being the first. The first alpine park earned on our own, the first
where we set a hiking goal and achieved it, the first where we walked where few
other people would ever walk, the first afternoon when we lolled in the hard-
earned glory of an August alpine meadow.

L. Landscapes

Mount Rainier dominates Puget Sound. If you doubt this, sit on the shore of
Lake Washington's Seward Park on a sunny afternoon and view the mountain
rising over the small city of Renton at the lake's southern end. You can't help
but feel its power. It seems to me that here and elsewhere in the American West
our vast spaces unite us: high desert, wide basins, broad seascapes, and snowy
alpine summits—wherever your perspective, what you see is a great expanse of
geography.

How you see this, however, has much to do with who you are. Jonathan
Raban, in his book *Passage to Juneau,* observes that Captain George Vancouver
saw the Northwest landscape at odds with the younger officers in his crew.
For Vancouver, who had come of age during the Enlightenment, landscape
was significant in how it would lend itself to husbandry. Of the Puget Sound

country, Vancouver wrote, "Our attention was immediately called to a landscape, almost as enchantingly beautiful as the most elegantly finished pleasure grounds of Europe." But Vancouver's younger officers were swept up in the then burgeoning Romantic Movement. In their journals they recorded towering escarpments, rocky cliffs, tumultuous tidewater passages, geographies filled with awe and dread—and decidedly uncivilized. Archibald Menzies, the botanist who accompanied Vancouver, wrote of an anchorage in Desolation Sound: ". . . there was a beautiful Waterfall which issued from a Lake close behind it & precipitated a wide foamy stream into the Sea over a shelving rocky precipice of about thirty feet high, its wild romantic appearance aided by its rugged situation & the gloomy forests which surrounded it." (I have visited this place and today it is much as it was when Menzies observed it.) Raban concludes that it was as if "Menzies and Vancouver, aboard the same ship at the same time in the same place, were on separate journeys through two landscapes." Wallace Stegner notes in his collection of essays, *Where the Bluebird Sings to the Lemonade Springs,* that the first European landscape artists never succeeded in capturing the aridity and scale of the West: they unfailingly made it look like Europe or the Hudson River Valley; the grandiosity of the West escaped them even though it lay just beyond the back side of their easels. Stegner goes on to say that nothing prepared Northern Europeans and Atlantic Americans for the American West, not their common law, not their belief in man's stewardship of the earth, not their faith in the yeoman farmer. If place shapes us, and I believe it does, it is also true that our other life experiences shape how we see place, where we were raised, the prevailing views of our compatriots, our religious inclinations, and even the language we speak.

M. Memories, Photographs, Mowich Lake

My family has spent so many weekends and taken so many photographs at Mount Rainier, I often lose track of what is memory, what is photograph. One of my earliest memories is of Longmire Campground where my father, my Aunt Harriet, and I, perhaps the weekend in June 1949 when my brother, Charlie, was born, had a picnic. Was this also a photograph?

But I have for certain a Kodachrome slide of my mother Natalie Mathison in the same campground taken in 1951. She's standing at one end of a picnic table and she's cooking on a green Coleman camp stove. She's wearing a pale-yellow cotton dress; her jacket is wool, a Hudson's Bay checkerboard pattern of red and white blocks identical to a jacket my father had; her hair is done up in a knot of double black braids; she is thirty-three. Behind Mother, you can see my parent's walk-in canvas and plywood trailer that was painted gray on top, had a thin red waistband stripe, and a dark green bottom and a profile that was rounded in front with a rear-end swooping out in back like a ducktail haircut. I can hear the bacon sizzling and feel the morning sun on my face and hear my brother chasing through the campsite and hear my father admonishing him to kick up less dust, but what I hear and smell and feel is certainly a memory, not a photograph.

Another photo is of my brothers Charlie and D and my sister Charlotte and I leaping from fallen log to fallen log to fallen log in the rainforest twilight of Ipsut Creek campground. It must be May—my father liked to camp in Ipsut Creek in May, before the snow was clear from the higher elevations. I remember that day and I remember the logs and I remember sailing from one log to another as if freed from the bonds of gravity.

I have a favorite photo of my father, at Mowich Lake in 1972. The photo is how I like to remember him: outdoors, robust, contemplative. We have just finished a hike to Spray Park. My father is wearing his black-leather hiking boots, redolent with the mink oil he used to waterproof them (boots with steel Triconi cleats that sometimes sparked when he hiked across the talus rock), a pair of Bermuda shorts, a short-sleeve plaid shirt, a stained Stetson cowboy hat. His ice ax rests between his knees. He is sitting on a log next to a young woman—my ex-wife—and she has long, suntanned legs, dark auburn hair, and the unabashed and effortless beauty of a twenty-two-year-old woman, but in this photo she looks tired and slightly annoyed and I wonder if she is already discomfited with our marriage, although I would not know this for another year.

N. Nevado del Ruiz

On the thirteenth of November 1985, twenty-three thousand residents of the town of Armero, Columbia, located one hundred miles west of Bogotá, perished in mudflows caused when the Andean volcano Nevado del Ruiz erupted. It was South America's worst volcanic tragedy. Two things about Nevado del Ruiz fascinate me. The first is that despite this being a relatively minor eruption, the twenty million cubic meters of hot ash and pyroclastic flows that spewed directly on the volcano's icecap was more than enough to trigger lahars that streaked down the sides of the volcano, until, four hours later, the lahars drowned Armero nearly sixty miles distant. It was mud that killed, not lava or volcanic gasses or ash or tephra or any of the other more dramatic phenomena. The second thing that fascinates me is that this was not the first time Nevado del Ruiz killed. In 1595, shortly after the Spanish conquest, and again in 1845 nearly identical eruptions destroyed Armero, each time with more loss of life. But each time the residents forgot, each time the residents rebuilt. There is in this lack of perspicacity something tragically human. Or is it something essentially human? A stubborn perseverance, a destiny to carry on despite our planet's dangerous history?

O. Ohanapecosh, Old Growth, and Conifers

What makes Ohanapecosh on the southeastern corner of Rainier National Park so memorable? I would say trees: old-growth conifers—Douglas fir, Western red Cedar, hemlock, some a thousand years old. There's also a lack of dense underbrush and a sparkling snowmelt-and-spring-fed river that runs through the campground, free of the glacial silt that muddies most Rainier rivers. My father liked to camp in Ohanapecosh in the late spring, often on Memorial Day, because, like Ipsut Creek, the campground was at a relatively low altitude and would be free of snow, but also, unlike Ipsut Creek, because it was at the far southeastern corner of the park where the spring weather would be drier. Even in the fifties Ohanapecosh was popular. By July you would have to arrive before noon to find a spot. The last time I camped there, in the mid-1980s, I was startled to see a reader-board under a row of flashing incandescent bulbs, its message in large black letters reading, WARNING! CAMPGROUND THIEVES!

The evolution of our National Parks—some would say the abuse of our National Parks—is well documented, as is the role of park rangers devolving from naturalist guides to police officers, as well as what many see as a declining consensus among Americans as to what the role of the parks should be. Each year, the Park Service closes more and more of the parks to automobiles, citing lack of funding, an agenda that has, I suspect, as much to do with protecting the parks from the people as it does saving the people's money. Each year, the Park Service institutes more and more rigorous steps you must follow—lotteries and waiting lists and arbitrary closures—in order to camp, hike, or climb. Each year Park Service employees seem to become dourer and dourer toward their visitors. Nevertheless, I am sympathetic to the Park Service's plight. I admire the determination of the park personnel to protect their charges, and I even understand the frustration they must feel at an increasingly urban and often careless clientele. But I prefer not to bemoan the decline of the parks. I passionately believe they are worth the trouble to visit, and I have made certain, raising my son John, that he has visited almost all of the major parks in the American West. Still, I'm glad I grew up in a time when visiting the parks was a spontaneous pastime, when you could, on a Friday afternoon, pack up your gear and head east, bound for any campground or any trail and a weekend in what was then your own backyard paradise.

P. Pompey and the Pyroclastic

The first time I visited Naples was in 1968 as a midshipman aboard the Navy destroyer *USS Bigelow*. My shipboard buddy and fellow-midshipman Parker Consaul and I blew off a trip to Pompeii opting instead for a bus ride up Mount Vesuvius. What I remember is sulfurous fumes, a gray nondescript crater, and an outdoor café where the wine was so bad Parker and I agreed it must have been diluted with ox blood. Nearly forty years later, my wife Susan, my son John, and I visited Rome and the Amalfi Coast. We set aside a morning for Pompeii. It was April and there were flowers—I hadn't expected flowers—and there were grassy slopes surrounding the Pompeian amphitheatre and there were palm trees and cypress trees and doorways whose lintels framed Vesuvius. I was intrigued by the Pompeian crosswalks, stepping stones at a height just below the axel height of Pompeian chariots. But it wasn't until I reached a nondescript storage shed with a high, corrugated metal roof that I appreciated the tragedy of Pompeii. Here were row upon row of the lesser artifacts: friezes that had hung over doorways, amphorae, pottery bowls, white stone sculptures of nymphs and fauns, faded wall frescoes not preserved well enough to warrant a place in the Museo Archeologico in Naples. But also here, in cases that resembled glass-sided coffins, stacked one on top of another, were the plaster casts of bodies, the victims of pyroclastic flow and tephra fall, crouched in the fetal positions where Vesuvius in its fiery fury had buried them at last.

Q. Quietude

When you drive south from Seattle on I-5, having left behind the skyscrapers and the harrowing traffic of the city, the interstate passes east of Boeing Field and then rises in a wide, sweeping turn, where, the solemn, silent immensity of Mount Rainier suddenly presents itself. Despite its quietude, for me seeing the mountain at this place is akin to hearing a great passage of music—the "Hallelujah" Chorus, Beethoven's "Ode to Joy," Brubeck, the Beatles, the Rolling Stones. I feel lighter, as if the cares of the day have fallen away, as if, despite all its travail, I see once again that at the heart of the universe there is a haunting beauty.

This face of the mountain is the face most familiar to me—I grew up not far from this spot, in McMicken Heights, the hill west of I-5 and east of SEATAC Airport. It's the face I saw walking to school, standing guard as a school-crossing patrolman, playing touch football games, picking beans in the Kent Valley, fishing for salmon in Elliott Bay. It's the face I saw the day John Kennedy was shot, the day the Gulf of Tonkin incident took place, the day in April 1965 when an earthquake sent my high-school classmates and me streaming into our open-air hallways.

From this perspective, Little Tahoma stands east of the nearly symmetrical summit—an august white in any season, the summit rises to fourteen thousand feet and then falls abruptly west to the six-thousand-foot crest of the Cascade Mountain Range. I can draw this profile with my eyes closed. In the darkest times of my life, during the breakup of a marriage, during my long naval deployments to Vietnam, during the death of my father, this was the view that reassured me by its continuity, by its silence, by its sameness.

Yet a paradox exists: the mountain is a geological newcomer, only a million years of age, a Pleistocene and Holocene phenomena, that can and most certainly will change its shape in the proximate future, and that is not, geologically speaking, a particularly good symbol of continuity.

But knowing this does not change my view.

R. Ring of Fire

If you trace your finger on a map of the Pacific Ocean, beginning in New Zealand, drawing it north over New Caledonia and northwest over New Guinea, and detour west to include all of the arc of Indonesia and then north up to the Philippines and north again to the Japanese home islands—Kyushu, Honshu, and Hokkaido— and over the Kamchatka Peninsula, and west across Alaska's Aleutian Island tail, continue onto the mainland and down over Mount Elias, and further down the Pacific coast—over Baker, Glacier Peak, Rainier, Adams, St. Helens, Hood, Crater Lake, and Shasta—until you reach the highlands of Mexico, Guatemala, Honduras, El Salvador, Nicaragua, and Costa Rica, bridge the isthmus at Panama, and follow the Andean backbone of South America over Columbia, Ecuador, Peru, Chile, all the way to the southern tip of the Tierra del Fuego, you will have traveled by fingertip around the Ring of Fire, where the subduction under continents of the ocean plates generates heat, which in turn melts the planet's crustal rock, which becomes magma, which forces its way up to the earth's surface and spills out as volcanoes, and which creates a landscape that from tropical jungle to icy Alaska peninsula is familiar to us by its pediments and escarpments and the conical cones of its peaks and in the restless and violent nature of its character.

S. St. Helens

In 1980, Mount St. Helens blew its top, the biggest volcanic eruption in the continental United States since Europeans began to record North American history. In that year I was thirty-three. By then I'd spent countless weekends camping and hiking below Mount Rainier as well as below most of the other Cascade volcanoes. I traveled most of the summers of my childhood throughout the American West where the evidence of volcanism was everywhere—in the bubbling mud pots of Yellowstone, in the sulfurous fumaroles of Lassen Peak, in the lava tubes of Idaho's Craters of the Moon. I'd even lived in Hawaii where I'd flown to the Big Island and hiked beside an active lava flow and watched it spill hissing and steaming into the Pacific Ocean. And yet I relegated volcanism to a distant province. When St. Helens blew I was as shocked as anybody living in Kansas or New York City. St. Helen's lateral blast mowed down six-foot-diameter Douglas firs, its ashfall covered twenty-two thousand square miles of the American West, its pyroclastic flows reached fifteen hundred degrees and sped at one hundred to one hundred fifty miles per hour, its lahars choked the Toutle River all the way to the Columbia. Until Mount St. Helens blew, I don't think I understood that *dormant* didn't mean *dead*. But what I also find interesting is that despite hearing the volcano erupt (I was aboard my sailboat off Puget Sound's Blake Island), despite my brother Charlie's first-hand observation of St. Helens moments after its side blew open (Charlie was hiking on the south side of Rainier National Park), despite the ashfall that dusted our cars, despite the breathless news coverage, despite the phone calls from our corporate brethren in the east asking if we were okay, despite the video of the news photographer running (unsuccessfully) from the volcano's pyroclastic fury, despite the fifty-seven deaths, despite the closure of Interstate 5 between Seattle and Portland, we felt an imperative in the days and weeks after the eruption to "get back to normal"; to ignore what had happened; to turn it off, if you will; to get on with our jobs, our love affairs, our vacations, our lives as we then saw them; to deny the spectacular and unsettling manifestation of St. Helens's eruption, and in this imperative I wonder if we were invoking yet another inborn survival technique, one needed to continue our lives on such a fragile and perilous planet, the technique of ignoring what we can't do anything about.

T. Trails, Flowers, Bears

My brother, Charles, tells of a morning in Moraine Park on the northwest flank of Rainier some years ago when he and his climbing buddy, Dave Thackeray, were breaking camp. Dave had climbed higher up a steep meadow so as to get one last picture of Rainier framed by meadow flowers. On his way back down, leaping over hummocks and logs like a skier in a mogul field, Dave landed on top of a sleeping bear. My brother, observing this from below, reports that Dave jumped in one direction, the bear in the other, and then the bear began to somersault, somersaulting head over tail down the meadow, somersaulting through the campsite, and then somersaulting over the edge of the meadow and down into the steep, forested ravine below. The bear, as far as my brother could tell, was physically unharmed but was no doubt traumatized.

In those days my brother and Dave were extraordinarily fit. They would often set off on a traverse, eschewing trails, plotting a path directly across the high country with no more guide than a topographic map and their copies of Fred Becky's *Cascade Alpine Guide*. They were mountaineering in the tradition of the Robert Redford movie *Jeremiah Johnson* (although without the pursuing Native American assassins). If there's such a thing as a mountaineer polity, my brother and Dave were part of it, its character being one of independence, spirituality, free thinking, self-reliance, cooperation. These traits, I think, can also be found in mountain cultures—the Swiss, the Tibetans, the Nepalese. And at one time they could be found in the mountain-climber culture everywhere, as typified by the Northwest climbing clubs like the Mountaineers and the Mazamas, as personified by such icons as the New Zealander, Sir Edmund Hilary, and the American, Jim Whittaker. But the contemporary climbing polity, in my view, has veered away from these values into a culture too often characterized by recklessness and self-aggrandizement, more interested in notoriety over independence, thrill-seeking over spirituality, risk-taking over self-reliance.

U. Under the Volcano

Of serious novels that feature volcanoes as a thematic element, perhaps none is better known than Malcolm Lowry's mid-twentieth-century novel *Under the Volcano*, (which was also a John Ford film starring Albert Finney and Jacqueline Bisset). I find Lowry's syntax difficult—it's a long journey from each sentence beginning to each sentence end and I sometimes have trouble remembering where the sentence started—but I admire his beautiful and precise descriptions of the land and the denseness of the settings he creates, which are rich in the atmosphere of the Valley of Mexico where the novel is set, and which also reflect the interior tribulations of the novel's characters. Lowry explores sexual betrayal, alcoholism (with which, sadly, he was all-too familiar), and the difficulty of forgiveness and reconciliation. In the book, Geoffrey and Yvonne Firmin are a couple estranged but drawn to each other even though they can't find the terms to forgive each other. In this, of course, there's a parallel to the volcanoes that preside over the story, Popocatépetl and Iztaccíhuatl, who are, in Aztec legend, lovers locked in a destructive affair but who cannot bear to be out of each other's sight.

There is, as far as I know, no authorial equivalent to Lowry for Mount Rainier, or even a popular fiction equivalent, as Raymond Chandler is to Los Angeles, or Tony Hillerman is for the Navajo and Pueblo southwest, or Jack London is for San Francisco.

Although there should be.

V. Vulcan

The Roman god of volcanoes, Vulcan—his Greek incarnation is Hephaestus—plays a surprisingly pedestrian role in Greco-Roman myth. He resides on the Sicilian island of Volcano, where he labors over his steaming forge as the armorer to the gods. He stars in no myth of his own. Deformed and lame and badly scarred as he is, however, he remains attractive to women: in some myths husband to Aphrodite (who eventually dumps him), in others to one of the Three Graces—there must be more than fire in Vulcan's forge.

Throughout time and geography, in the mythology of volcanoes, sex is often a theme—in Hawaii, Pele manifests as a beautiful and jealous young woman, hazardous to all her lovers; in Mexico, Popocatépetl and Iztaccíhuatl, who inspired Lowry's novel; in the Philippines, the volcano Mayon, said to have been created by divine intervention on behalf of a princess and her lover; in Indonesia, Tengger, the result of an ogre's unrequited love. Perhaps something in the heat and violence of volcanoes is analogous to sex: passion to flame, loss of control to eruptions.

Of course, not all volcano myths bear on sex. In Iceland volcanoes are seen as a deterrent to island invaders. In Greek creation myths, they are the graveyard for giants who, having challenged the gods and lost, were punished by being buried alive under Mount Etna where, according to Bullfinch, "Their breath comes up through the mountain, and is what men call the eruption of the volcano."

W. Weather

Rainier makes its own weather.

I recall one August Saturday over thirty years ago when I accompanied a girlfriend up to Paradise Park. Although the woman was originally from Kansas, she then lived in Seattle and was taking a climbing course prior to attempting an ascent of the mountain, the ascent I suppose a way to establish her claim as a Puget Sounder. I was at the time living in San Diego, where I'd spent the previous four months living on a sailboat and cruising Mexico and Southern California waters. Now, since I was about to run out of money, I was back in the Northwest looking for a job. My girlfriend's climbing course was to take most of the day—I don't know why she asked me along—perhaps she felt guilty. At the time (and during the course of our relationship) she always dated other men, and she always struggled to fit me in. On this occasion I didn't mind. I'd spent the spring and summer at sea level and I was anxious to log time in the mountains. I'd packed a light lunch in my daypack, thrown in my Gore-Tex jacket, but otherwise wore only a T-shirt, cotton shorts, and a pair of good hiking boots. The day was sunny and warm. I set out on the Skyline Trail. The trail begins at the Paradise Inn, ascends flowered meadows, rises above the tree line, follows the ridge above the Nisqually glacier until it reaches Panorama Point, beyond which perpetual snowfields begin and the climbers' trail departs up to Camp Muir. By the time I reached Panorama Point I could see that clouds had already welled up from the south and west. Perhaps it would have been wiser to turn back. But I hadn't been this high since the winter ski season—the trail at this point is nearly eight thousand feet—and I wanted to complete the loop and follow the trail to Golden Gate and pass below the Paradise Glacier's snout and then cross the Paradise River at Sluiskin Falls and then continue back to the visitor center parking lot without retracing my steps or prematurely descending into the meadows. Within fifteen minutes, however, I was enveloped in clouds, all the more dangerous because I was crossing a snowfield marked only by cairns. Thunder pealed. Rain began to fall. Then the wind came up. To my shock, it began to snow. Was this August? My Gore-Tex jacket was no longer water-repellant. (Later I learned that during my four months of saltwater sailing salt crystals had lodged between its "breathable" threads.) I doubled my pace. But despite hiking as fast as I dared—the "white-out" conditions of falling snow, a snowfield underfoot, and fog made it difficult to see the trail—I began to tremble uncontrollably. By the time I reached Golden Gate and its shortcut back to Paradise, the snow had given way to rain and the snowfield to a snow-free trail but I was in the early grip of hypothermia with an hour's descent still left to go. My girlfriend found me huddled before the fireplace in Paradise Inn, sipping a cup of coffee. In her climbing class, a thousand feet lower on the mountain, where she practiced her rope-ups, her glissades, and her ice ax arrests, it hadn't even rained.

X. Xenophobia

My brothers and sister and I always pitied our Pennsylvania cousins: they had to live in Pennsylvania. When I went back east to college in Maryland, I missed the West even though over time I grew fond of the Chesapeake Bay, fond of the skipjack oyster boats, fond of the brick and cobblestone towns of the Eastern Shore, fond of the museums and monuments of Washington, D.C. But fondness is not love. I never grew fond of the absence of mountains. Easterners say they have mountains: the Blue Ridge, the Adirondacks, the Appalachians. Any Westerner knows better. Where are the glacial cirques, the basalt towers, the ragged escarpments, the ice-sculpted valleys? Where are the perpetual snowfields, the conifer-covered ridges, the meadows flowered by blossoms? Above all, where are the volcanoes? It seemed to me that there was something dissolute about a place with no volcanoes, as if the land had grown tired and had lost its vigor and had begun to sag away.

As Westerners, we live in a geologically young land, a land where mountains grow taller and rivers run faster, where oceanic plates subduct under North America and lift an entire third of the continent. This lifting is why our land is so restless, is the root cause of our seismic hazards, of our earthquakes and our geothermal instabilities, of our volcanic explosiveness. But it is also the root cause of our land's beauty, of its sweeping basins, its snow-clad peaks, its tumultuous rivers, its glaciated summits, its high plains and its high prairies, the vertiginous escarpments of its shorelines, the lofty green meadows of its mountain ranges. To live amid such beauty you pay a price. As a Westerner, you know the price is worth paying.

Y. Yellowstone

It's June 2007 and my son, my wife, and I have just entered the West Entrance of Yellowstone National Park. In a few miles we'll cross the rim of the Yellowstone Caldera and enter one of the most volcanically active regions on the planet. (Once we would have called it "geothermally active," which sounds so much safer. Now we know better.) The night before, we camped along the Madison River, above Earthquake Lake, formed in the 1959 Hebgen Lake Earthquake, a 7.5 Richter whopper that triggered a landslide that dammed the Madison River and that took the lives of fifty-nine campers. (Although last night I was worried less about seismicity and more about bears—a note on the campground reader board warned of grizzly sightings; we were sleeping in a tent, which my son and I had pitched at the edge of the nearly empty campground in a field of knee-deep, indigo-blue lupine).

I've visited Yellowstone five times, the first in 1949, again in 1956 and 1962, the last with John and Susan in 1999. Its power entrances me: geysers, boiling springs, mud pots, the pervasive pong of sulfur. But I also like Yellowstone's sense of space, as if you are standing on top of the world. In a sense, you are. The park lies at over six thousand feet on a volcanic plateau formed by one of the deepest lava flows in the world, as much as twelve hundred feet deep, and it straddles the Continental Divide. Today, during our drive through the park, we'll cross the Divide several times.

It wasn't until the 1960s and 1970s that USGS geologists figured out that most of Yellowstone was actually a giant caldera—the enormous crater of a collapsed volcano below which magma still pooled. The volcano had collapsed 630,000 years ago in an eruption so intense that it was twenty-five hundred times more powerful than the eruption of Mount St. Helens. The event spewed ash over all of North America, caused the extinction of numerous North American species (and may have threatened the near-extinction of our own species), and was the third such eruption in the last two million years. Since then, the caldera has spawned lesser eruptions at fairly frequent and geologically recent intervals as evidenced by lesser craters and extensive lava flows. We now know that Yellowstone is a stratovolcano, one of such enormous magnitude that the geophysicists have coined a new term for it: *supervolcano.* What's more, there is absolutely no question that the Yellowstone supervolcano will erupt again. The supervolcano sits atop the Yellowstone Hot Spot, a plume of magma that rises up from the earth's mantle. The hot spot doesn't move. But the North American Plate does. Over the last seventeen million years the plate moving over the magma plume has spewed a path of destruction across Washington, Oregon, California, Nevada, Idaho, and now Wyoming. At the present time the plume feeds a series of magma chambers scattered throughout the region, the largest and greatest of which are now under the Yellowstone plateau. The plateau floor is rising at a rate of a half-inch per year. The rate of expansion has been accelerating. The USGS regards the threat serious enough to warrant an extensive monitoring system of borehole strain meters, tilt meters, steam sample gauges, and extensive and continuing testing of hot spring effluent. So far the USGS website claims there's no case for a near-term eruption (although some non-USGS scientists dispute this). But even if there was an eruption, compared to other volcanically active areas, like Puget Sound, Yellowstone has a relatively sparse population. Presumably there would be sufficient time before any significant eruption to close the park, as the area around St. Helens was closed in 1980 (although not closed enough to prevent the fifty-seven deaths that did occur). This reassurance of course doesn't address the really *big* eruptions, the species-extinction eruptions.

As far as Susan, John, and I are concerned, before our Yellowstone day is out, we will watch geysers erupt, photograph emerald-green hot springs, share a picnic lunch on the shores of Yellowstone Lake, and savor the scale of this place, its sense of limitlessness and possibility, its open horizons where the sun seems brighter and the clouds seem taller, its wide-open westernness. But later, after we leave, perhaps we'll ponder Yellowstone's other lesson: that the earth evolves by catastrophes just as often as it evolves gradually.

Z. Zero

In 1985, when my wife Susan and I were on the cusp of moving to Hong Kong, a friend, Marty Waite, presented us with a photograph of Mount Rainier. "Don't forget us," he said. There was zero chance of that. We hung the photo in one of our Hong Kong flat's bathrooms, so that every day amid the sweltering Hong Kong heat, we would see the mountain's cool beauty.

Chance plays the greatest role in determining where we ultimately call home. We never know what decision or what chance act made the choice irrevocable.

The passion I have for my native Northwest might well have been spent on other places. Certainly others were as probable: Pennsylvania where both my parents grew up (they might never have come west); Southern California, where in 1949 my father's aerospace profession was centered; even Brazil, where I was born. But if fate brought me to the Northwest, it was my own resolve that brought me back. After six years in Hong Kong, followed by a one-year hiatus in California, Susan and I (and by then our son John, who had been born Hong Kong) returned to the Northwest.

There's zero chance we'll leave again. The Northwest is in our bones. We like to breathe its air. We like to hear its rains drumming on our roof. We like to smell the cleansing scent of its Douglas fir. We like to wake up amid the majesty of ice-capped peaks. We like to witness its volcano dawns. It is our drug—addictive, mind altering, shaping how we see everything, how we see God.

I grew up under a volcano not thinking it a volcano.

But it was.

It still is.

And I'm different because of it.

Wooden Boat

THIS MAY MORNING THE HARBOR below our Friday Harbor house blushes pink. Scoter ducks scribe inky Vs through strands of kelp shaped like question marks. Across the channel, on Brown Island, the sun gilds the Douglas firs. In town—we can see it from our front deck—at the foot of Front Street, a green and white Washington State ferry loads its cars. Were it March, we might be among its passengers, but today, and for the rest of the spring and summer, my wife Susan, our fourteen-year-old son John, and I will commute by boat, our own wooden boat, which lies at our dock, suspended from its mooring whips, ready to skim the meanders and whirls and eddies of the morning tide. The boat is twenty feet long, hull black, topsides white and tan, her teak trim varnished—"bright" as we wooden-boat people call it.

We had the boat built expressly for this purpose: to deliver us safely, at high speed, and with some style from the mainland to our island retreat and back.

* * *

"A wooden boat," the builders of our boat say on their Nexus Marine website, "has an indefinable beauty of line that is difficult or impossible to produce by molding or bending thin sheets of metal."

After all, the line of trunk and branch is among the most harmonious in nature.

And there's depth in wood, especially varnished wood—you can see inside it.

Wood perfumes the air with its resins—who hasn't, on a summer's day, lingered in the fragrance of a lumberyard?

Wood is naturally buoyant—you feel it in the way a wooden boat lifts on a wave, as if it were alive—and it *has* been alive, and remains alive in a way that fiberglass or aluminum never can be.

But wood is not for everybody, not for the capricious or the impatient or the hard-riding or the owner with a thin wallet. Varnish wears under the sun; teak abrades; paint fades; dings mar the perfection of brightwork. Wood's longevity depends on the care you choose to lavish on it. A wooden boat, like a human being, is a brief, ephemeral flare of energy amid the cosmic slide to disorder and darkness, its very perishability part of its attraction (at least for some of us), a declaration of independence against the travails of time.

* * *

I began my love affair with wooden boats on a jet-lagged summer leave in 1988. Susan and I were living in Hong Kong—I was managing a computer sales subsidiary—but we had retained a Seattle houseboat as a home-leave retreat. I remember a July-bright afternoon, half-drunk from jet-lag, jogging over to the Wooden Boat Shop (now gone) on the other side of Lake Union's Portage Bay where I spotted a cold-molded, wood-epoxy pram, its hull white, its interior a herringbone of cedar strips, its lines as neat as a cockle shell. I bought her on the spot and rowed her home. When we relocated back to Seattle, I moved her up to Friday Harbor where I would launch her from our dock and row her around Brown Island, and where, when her plywood bow began to delaminate, I cut out the rotted and splayed wood and, with epoxy and filler, laid in a replacement bow, a project well beyond my woodworking skills, but in which I found relief from the agonies of the "downsizing" of the electronics company where I then worked. I liked the feel of the wood under my hands. I liked it that with epoxy and resin I could "heal" my little boat. I liked bringing the grain of the cedar back to life under coats of varnish followed by sanding followed by more varnish, so that in the end I could look deep into the wood, and so that when I rowed the boat, I felt as if I was floating inside a bowl of maple syrup. My work wasn't perfect. There were sags in the varnish. Too much filler masked the grain. I could voyage in Friday Harbor but it would never carry me farther than that. But by my labor, I became invested in my boat.

When it was time to find a boat that could take us from the mainland to the San Juans, I went to the Nexus Marine boathouse located on the slough-laced delta of the Snohomish River among pilings that were once log booming grounds and moorings for fishing boats. The building is two-story, yellow-planked, and barn-shaped with a high, exposed-rafter interior and open on one side to the river. There's a "buzz-and-walk-in" bell. When you slide the door open, you enter a mote-softened, high-raftered space populated with big table saws and drill presses, and beyond the saws you'll see another door that is the entrance to the owners'—David and Nancy's—apartment. In the boathouse you may feel as I do: that you've stepped into Ratty or Mole's house in *The Wind in the Willows*.

David is usually wearing jeans and boots and a carpenter's smock and is out in one of the several rooms of the boathouse, which David and Nancy call "the shed," amid plastic curtains and drying lights and boat jigs and racks of lumber that make you feel as if you're wandering in a maze. David is medium height and has just reached the age of sixty. A gray beard frames high cheekbones and bright eyes. He's attentive to everything, answering only after considering what he is about to say, and then speaking in perfectly formed sentences. He laughs in sudden tenor bursts. David reminds me of a department store Santa Claus despite the fact that he is trim and a long-distance cyclist and a vegetarian and a congregant in good standing at his Everett temple. In the sixties, David dropped out of Cornell Engineering. He joined the army. On his discharge, he toured Europe on a motorcycle.

Nancy, who likes to call herself a reformed hippie, still has a hippie's long, straight hair, a certain joy-in-life innocence, and a deep-contralto laugh that disarms you and draws you in. She is short and sturdy and as ready as David is to pick up a tool belt or a varnish brush. Like David she is unusually attentive to what you say—Nancy never fails to respond with a ready quip. She calls all the boats Nexus has built her "babies." Before meeting David, Nancy was a theatrical director and set builder and a builder of other theatrical props. Later she and David went to Alaska where they fished for salmon in Bristol Bay.

"We fished," Nancy says, "so we could afford to build boats."

And, after Alaska, they did build boats—rowboats and dories and outboards and sailboats. Wooden boats. Beautiful boats.

* * *

As in any definition of beauty, the essence is illusive. David maintains that nautical beauty is "hind mind," originating in our reptilian brains, and that people are genetically programmed to recognize it, but he also says that the lines of

NEIL MATHISON

the most beautiful boats mirror their movement through the water. Sheer, for example, is the line from the bow to the stern at the top edge of the hull: it's often shaped like the wave left behind by the hull's passage. On a Nexus boat, the high bow is designed to rise in steep-pitched Puget Sound seas while at the same time keeping the boat dry. The low stern insures tracking in following seas and at slow trolling speeds. Each shape is derived from what the boat is supposed to do. In David's view, function always drives design.

"All boats," David says, "are workboats."

But David also says that the nature of wood predicates design. Wood must be bent and when it bends it bends in fair curves. Marine-grade lumber is fine-grained and straight, like a Douglas fir tree trunk is straight, and the most elegant boat designs draw upon this trait of the lumber.

The best designers design like David, unveiling what is already in their materials. You hear this in the vocabulary of boat building. *Dead rise* is how flat or V-shaped the bottom of the hull is. *Waterlines* are imaginary horizontal slices cut bow to stern. *Tumblehome* is the inclination of a boat's sides where the sides meet the deck. *Dead rise, tumblehome, waterline*: in the sound of the words, you almost hear the shapes of the boats.

* * *

During the winter of 1995 to 1996, frame by frame, stringer by stringer, our boat took shape. Finally one day Nancy called. "Have you picked a name?" A date had been set for our boat's launching.

The name we chose was *Ceilidh*, pronounced KAY-lee, a Celtic word for a party where whiskey flows and pipers play, where friends gather and drink and laugh and sing, where everybody tells each other lies, which was not unlike the party we convened the night we launched *Ceilidh*, at eleven in the evening, when the August tide was sufficiently high to float her off her ways, a night which, as it turned out, was also Susan's fortieth birthday. The birthday limo, loud with its celebrants, arrived at the Nexus boathouse. Our guests spilled out, bearing their bottles of wine and their plastic cups of margaritas. Susan broke a magnum of champagne over the bow. John and I manned the cockpit. The Nexus crew winched us down until we settled into the Snohomish River light and dry and free floating at last, as if *Ceilidh* was coming to life, or perhaps returning to life, the wood within her, once afloat, resurrected.

* * *

The first few years after *Ceilidh's* launching defined an era when our family was young and our friends' families were young. Back then, summer was theatre and *Ceilidh* was our stage and we were impresarios organizing kids, tubes, knee boards, fishing rods, skis, tents, stoves, folding chairs, and portable barbecues.

But even back then *Ceilidh* was more than a vehicle for play.

Ceilidh was where my dad and I shared our last boat ride before he died.

Ceilidh was where my brother, Charlie, and I sought solace after Dad's death by fishing on the west side of San Juan Island amid a pod of orcas, Charlie landing a salmon, the orcas diving around us, their flanks mirroring *Ceilidh's* black and white hull, the orcas and us and all the world alive in the shadow of Dad's death.

Ceilidh's beauty can still catch your breath. Strangers often approach us. *Your boat,* they say, *we've admired for years.* The staff at the marina where we keep *Ceilidh* call it "our Nexus," investing it with extra care as they launch and retrieve her. Once, post 9/11, we were chased by the US Coast Guard, for no other reason as it turned out than to get a better look at our boat.

This is the boat we asked David and Nancy to build.

By having it built, were we nautically preening?

Or simply proclaiming ourselves to be alive, an announcement of our presence in the world?

* * *

On this May morning in Friday Harbor, however, I'm not fretting about preening.

The outboard engine is idling. Susan has wiped the dew from the windscreen. John is casting off the spring lines and the mooring whip lines. I throw the throttle in reverse. John pushes off and steps aboard. I back to the end of our dock. I spin the wheel. I shift the engine into forward gear. We motor out into the channel between Brown Island and San Juan Island.

The conical hat of Mount Baker rears up this morning looking like a volcanic strawberry sundae. The windscreen is fogging up. I zip open the canvas window, roll it up, tuck it above my head. I check my jacket—zipped, slip on sunglasses, pull on a pair of polypro gloves, and palm the throttle forward. The boat rises on a plane, its bow pointed directly at Mount Baker, and we are off and swerving over the curlicues and meanders and boils, our speed over thirty knots, the boat skewing back and forth, a feeling so familiar I can almost guess where we are by each rip and whirlpool, just as the Salish Indians paddling their cedar canoes knew where they were by rip and whirlpool, but now we are slaloming around driftwood, flying across a world gilded and silvered and crimsoned by the sun, a world in such perfect balance I am, as always, nearly tearful at its beauty—or is it the wind that causes my eyes to tear?

We have made this passage a hundred times, each time different. This morning the speed and light and the crisp air are transformative, imbuing us and our boat with the splendor of this day, writing another day into our lives, into the very bones of our boat. And if anything was missing—the sunrise, Mount Baker, John or Susan or *Ceilidh*—then this morning would be less than it is. But it's all here. This morning everything is here.

Twenty-two Ways to Lose and (Maybe) Regain Paradise

1 The Facts

I'LL START WITH THE FACTS. Facts don't tell the whole story, don't address how to tell it, don't tell if it's too soon to tell it. Still, the facts are the story's bones. The facts are these: several summers ago, in 2006, in British Columbia's Desolation Sound, while sailing our sailboat *Allurea* in company with my sister's sailboat *Integrity*, my nephew, William G., then fifteen years old, was thrown from the bow of his dad's speeding inflatable dinghy. The dinghy was thirteen feet long. It had a powerful outboard motor. It was traveling over thirty miles per hour. They hit a submerged log. When Will surfaced, his right arm was gone, cut off by the dinghy's outboard propeller. His father pulled Will back onboard, pressed his hands against the severed stump of Will's arm (so as to arrest the bleeding), and sped back to Walsh Cove on West Redonda Island where our two sailboats were rafted together. For the next three and a half hours, we waited for the Canadian Coast Guard to evacuate Will. Eventually they did.

Those are the facts.

2 The Context

The fact that Will lost his arm is a tragedy.

It is also a fact that the tragedy injured all our family members. If our losses were not as severe as Will's, we still lost something. Something vital. Not a limb. Not anything like what Will lost. But something important. Something essential to our peace and happiness and innocence. Something we may never regain again. Also, the facts don't give context. That Will was a young man of extraordinary athletic ability. Or that his sisters, Elizabeth, who was seventeen, and Catherine, who was ten, and his cousins—my son John, who was sixteen, and my brother's son Greg, who was fifteen, and my brother's daughter Alexandra, who was sixteen—were also present. Or that my sister's family and my family had made similar annual sailing trips for more than a dozen years together. Or that our children had grown up on boats. Or that this trip was a sort of valedictory before the oldest cousin, Elizabeth, went off to college. Or that my brother-in-law and my sister, and my wife Susan and I prided ourselves on being careful, cautious, and vigilant boaters. Or that this place, Walsh Cove, on Redonda Island was one of our favorite places on the planet.

Before the accident, Walsh Cove was a place of unqualified joy.

After the accident, I don't know what it is.

3 Why Walsh Cove Was Paradise

Walsh Cove lies on West Redonda Island, on Waddington Channel, just north of Desolation Sound, where Vancouver Island necks into the British Columbia mainland and forms a labyrinth of islands and passages. The cove is fjord country. Twelve thousand years ago the Cordillera Ice Sheet—the last great glaciation of the present ice age—sculpted this place. The islands are steep-sided, rocky-shored, conifer-clad, often snowcapped. The channels and passages are sometimes a thousand feet deep. On the mainland, even during the hottest summers, you see glaciers and snowfields. There are eagles everywhere. Also salmon. If you're inclined, you can catch big kings in Waddington Channel. Or you can harvest oysters from West Redonda's rocky shore. Or you can set traps in the deep center channel and pull up baskets of pink, tumbling, sweet-tasting shrimp. We often water ski here. The Inside Passage to the north blocks the cold Pacific tides, and snowmelt rivers lay freshwater over the top of saltwater so that the less dense freshwater floats on the saltwater, allowing the surface temperature to warm in summer to over seventy degrees. It can rain here—the cool, blue, luxuriant forest is evidence of the rain—but summers are drier than New York City. There are islets that not only protect the anchorage but provide cliffs for jumping into the cove's deep water, reefs suitable for swimming, and miniature archipelagos ideal for kayak and dinghy exploration. There are no mosquitoes. The summer dusk lasts until after ten o'clock. There are Indian petroglyphs on the cliffs. I have a snapshot of my dad that I took here in 1982: he's in a swimsuit, sunning himself on the bare rock on the Walsh Cove shore.

4 The Context of Time

We've been sailing in British Columbia for thirty years. For the last fifteen, we sailed with our children. In the beginning, we lashed child car seats to our backstays and strapped our infants into them, wove netting into our lifelines to prevent our toddlers from slipping overboard, watched our children learn to swim and ride tubes and master water skis. Because we come back every year, because we visit the same coves, the same harbors, the same midden beaches, we see our children in ways we might not otherwise see them. They form a tableau, all the more beautiful for its repetition. Except now the voyages remaining with our children are fewer than those made. Except where we once saw these places with unqualified joy, now we're not so certain.

5 The Scream

It's after dinner, eight o'clock. August 10, 2006. We're anchored in Walsh Cove, rafted with *Integrity*, stern lines ashore. The islands are conifer blue and the light is gold and the wind is still. My son John, my niece Alex, my nephew Greg, my wife Susan, and I are below deck on *Allurea* watching *The Man Who Would Be King*. My sister and her daughters Elizabeth and Catherine are next door on *Integrity*. A dinghy roars into the anchorage. We rock gently side-to-side. It's my brother-in-law. Why so fast in the anchorage?

Then my sister screams.

Neil! Will lost his arm!

6 On the Nature of Irreversibility

There are certain moments that are irreversible. Pearl Harbor. Hiroshima. The assassination of Martin Luther King. In our family, this is such a moment. When Will lost his arm. After which life will never be the same.

7 PTS

I'm at a Christmas party at my sister's Lake Washington house, four months after Will lost his arm. I'm talking with a psychologist friend of my sister's, a local celebrity, one of those people you sometimes connect with, although not in any significant way—she once owned a house we lived in; her daughter is a friend of my niece, Elizabeth; we've shared a glass of wine or two at our house in Sun Valley. She's thanking me for the support we'd provided Will and my sister and Will's dad the previous summer. I begin telling her about my sleeplessness and my dreams and how sometimes, recalling the accident, I'm overcome with nausea. The people who offer condolences, I said, rarely comprehend our horror. I tell her that I can't stop remembering: my sister's cry, Will's blood, the darkness, the long wait for the Coast Guard, the bungled attempt to move Will, the vigil after he and my sister left.

It sounds to me, she says, that you're suffering post-traumatic stress.

Her observation shocks me. Me? PTS?

In order to recover, she says, placing her hand briefly and gently on my shoulder, you'll have to confront your memories.

8 Statistics

The US Coast Guard Boating Safety website reports that in 2006 there were 710 boating deaths and 3,474 boating injuries despite a 2 percent decline in US boat registrations. There were 153 cases where the boat hit a floating object, seventy-two cases where the victim was ejected from the boat, 234 cases where the propeller struck the victim, 2,209 of the total cases occurred in open motorboats, 80 percent of which were less than sixteen feet in length.

The statistics are dry. No tears. No blood. No lost arms.

9 Mayday

We issue a *Mayday*. (Do I? Does Susan? Did my sister?)

In seconds a Canadian Coast Guardsman answers.

Regardless of who issued the call, I'm the one who replies. I stumble through our geographic coordinates, the situation with Will, the name of the cove, the necessity for medical evacuation.

Don't move the victim, they say. *Try to stop the bleeding,* they say. *Find the arm.*

10 Finding Will's Arm

My brother-in-law already knows that nobody can find Will's arm. (Later the doctors will tell us that because of the weight of bone and muscle tissue, the arm would have sunk to the bottom instantly). He also knows he can't tell his wife this, or his daughters this, or the armada of dinghies now assembling to find Will's arm this. Although I'm as close to Will's dad in this situation as anybody is, I can't imagine his agony. Will's dad leads the armada out into the dimming evening, a dozen dinghies, a couple dozen searchers. As darkness falls one dinghy will run out of gas, another's outboard will overheat. My nephew, Greg M., will be aboard the dinghy whose outboard overheats, a dinghy piloted by a stranger, a fact I discover only when I can't find him. Of course, nobody finds the arm.

11 Community

On the night of the accident, before the search for Will's arm, my nephew, Greg M., and I roar through the anchorage searching boat-by-boat for help. There are perhaps a dozen boats. We find two nurses, one of whom is semi-intoxicated, the other of whom is an emergency room specialist. We also find neighbors who offer medical supplies. At each stop, nurses and neighbors board their own dinghies and head for *Integrity* and *Allurea*. At our last stop, at the most distant end of the anchorage, perhaps two miles from where our boats are anchored, we find a retired doctor. The doctor and his charter-boat skipper board our dinghy. We speed back to Will. We don't know these people. They aren't members of our tribe. We'll never see them again. But on this night we form a single community, united in common cause, which is to keep this young man, this young American, Will G., alive.

12 Apocalypse

It's moonless. The Coast Guard radios us to turn on our lights. So we turn on lights—navigation lights, deck lights, steaming lights, spreader lights, spotlights, flashlights until we're lit up like a Fourth of July fireworks display, except we're not a fireworks display and what we resemble, it seems to me, is the scene in *Apocalypse Now* where Martin Sheen's riverboat passes under the bridge and the bridge is lit by flares and searchlights and all around the bridge there is darkness and danger and the Vietcong because the bridge is a false refuge of light just as we're a false island of light in a moonless night of darkness and at the heart of our darkness is a nightmare and the nightmare is Will, lying in the dinghy, covered with blankets and blood.

13 The Rescue

Three and a half hours after Will has lost his arm, a Coast Guard inflatable boat roars into the anchorage. They have detoured ten miles to retrieve a surgeon who overheard our plight on the radio and has volunteered to help. There's confusion. Who's supervising? I'm standing on *Integrity* playing a spotlight on Will who is still in the dinghy. I can see in the faces of the young Coast Guard men and women that none have seen an accident as grim as this. Nobody's holding the boats together. They start to lift Will into the Coast Guard boat and the boats skew apart and Will tips into the water. One doctor grabs Will's good arm and then someone else grabs Will's leg and together they haul Will back into the dinghy while Will screams in pain. One of the nurses—the semi-intoxicated nurse—falls backwards into the water. I'm shouting *Hold the goddamn dinghies together for Christ's sake!* But nobody listens. (And now I ask myself, why wasn't I holding the dinghies together?)

14 Blood

I never saw Will bleed. What I saw were the tracks of his blood. Blood on towels. Blood on blankets. Blood on teak decks. Blood on the PVC of the inflatable dinghy. The night of the accident, after my sister and Will had left with the Coast Guard (Will's dad staying behind with the boat and his daughters), after our neighbors had returned to their boats, after I turned out the lights, after John and Greg and Alex gathered up clean towels and unused blankets, it was Will's dad who gathered up the towels and blankets and swimsuits and sweatshirts that were soaked with Will's blood. A month later, when my brother, D., and I helped Will's dad bring *Integrity* back to Seattle, Will's dad was still cleaning up blood. Is this cleansing of blood a form of penitence? Is it one we owe because as fathers and mothers and aunts and uncles we're bound to keep our children safe and when we don't, even if we're blameless, we owe something? Will said in a speech that he delivered to the Puget Sound Blood Center on Valentine's Day 2008 that when he lost his arm the water turned "crimson." I can't imagine what Will's dad first thought, the water crimson with his son's blood. Later, at his high school in Seattle, Will captained the Varsity Blood Team. "My blood type is A negative," Will told his classmates. "A negative accounts for only 6 percent of the population. . . .Without a donor's blood," Will told them, ". . . I wouldn't be alive."

15 The Vigil

I promise Will's dad I will stand vigil by the VHF radio until Will is onboard the helicopter and my sister, who has accompanied Will in the Coast Guard inflatable, is on her way to the Campbell River Hospital. At one point they have to abort the airlift because "the subject," as they call Will in the desiccated parlance of first responders, has an "adverse" medical condition. I decide not to tell Will's dad this until the situation is stable. (Later we learn that Will was suffering hypothermia, his blood pressure dangerously low. Later I'll learn that Will's dad was also listening to the radio.)

On *Allurea* my crew has all fallen asleep. I can't sleep. (It is the first of many nights that I won't be able to sleep). I pour myself a glass of wine. The sky is lightening. We have planned an early departure. We're out of cell phone range in Walsh Cove and until we get in range, we won't know what has happened with Will. When I go topside Will's dad is already preparing to get underway. We cast off *Integrity*. We raise our own anchor. Slowly we motor out of the cove. Will we ever return?

Because my sister has accompanied Will, we've agreed with Will's dad to communicate by VHF radio so as to free the cell phones to receive my sister's call. It will take about an hour before we reach cell phone coverage. We follow *Integrity* as though losing sight of her might cause us to lose sight of her forever. Will's dad is pushing her hard. We can't keep up. The kids onboard *Allurea*, John, Alex, and Greg, wake up. Each asks about Will. We have nothing new to tell them. We hug each other, speak softly, offer to lend each other a hand. It seems as if we're in a dream, as if all we have to do is wake up and last night will go away. At the end of Waddington Channel, we pass the point where we should have cell coverage but we still haven't heard anything. We decide to call *Integrity* on VHF. Susan speaks into the microphone and then she hands it to me and I speak into the microphone. The radio remains silent. We expect the worst.

Finally the VHF crackles to life. It's Will's dad calling us from *Integrity*. Will is alive. Will is undergoing a second operation. Will has punctured a lung and broken his scapula but his spine appears to be okay. As it turns out, my sister has been unable to call. She and Will are in Vancouver at Children's Hospital and my sister is in a zone where cell phone calls are not permitted; a landline phone is unavailable. As soon as we hear Will's prognosis—he will make it—a weight lifts, but not all the weight.

We rendezvous at the Seattle Yacht Club Outstation in Cortes Bay. I book reservations for Will's dad and the girls to fly by float plane to Seattle. It's Catherine's tenth birthday. Before Will's dad and his daughters leave, Susan bakes a blackberry cobbler, hangs the Happy Birthday banner over *Integrity's* companionway. Just prior to the float planes departure, Will's dad receives word that alarms us: Will has a fever; they can't seem to get the fever down.

All the other club members are kind. All the club members are solicitous. All the other club members speak softly in our presence.

I can't wait to get out of there.

16 The Hug

The first time I see Will after the accident—it's six weeks after Will lost his arm—I hug him and he cries out in pain and I discover I've inadvertently squeezed his still-healing scar on the stump of his arm. At this point Will is just coming off the morphine. He's addicted, my sister says. In cases like Will's, the patient almost always becomes addicted. And then what you have to do, she says, is break the addiction.

17 Symmetry

There's a TV series that I've recently come to enjoy: it's called *Monk* and it's about a San Francisco detective named Adrian Monk who suffers from obsessive-compulsive disorder. Monk obsesses about lack of symmetry in everything: pictures that hang at crooked angles, parking meters that he has neglected to touch when he walks by, numbers of things that are odd when he prefers them even. In one episode, Monk goes to see a psychiatrist, not his usual psychiatrist, and the psychiatrist is missing an arm. The actor who plays Monk, Tony Shalhoub, does the most beautiful job capturing Monk's discomfort in the presence of an amputee. As the psychiatrist questions Monk, every one of Monk's answers contains the word "symmetrical." The episode is uncomfortable and funny and revealing of how people feel in the presence of an amputee. You have to wonder: Are we hard-wired to recoil from missing limbs? Will has developed an instinct for having his photo taken: he always stands so that you won't see his missing arm. But when I see Will, what I see is a reproach: How did we fail to keep our child safe? What happened to our prudence, our planning, our precautions?

18 Screen Saver

The screen saver on my computer is a photograph I took two days after Will lost his arm, after Will's dad and the girls have gone back to Seattle, after we've escaped the outstation, after we've slipped into a hazy hiatus between the horror of the accident and the continuation of our voyage. I'm not a particularly talented photographer but this snapshot, it seems to me, captures the nature of that evening. We're anchored in Squirrel Cove on Cortes Island. It's about seven o'clock. There are no people in the photo. The American flag on *Allurea's* stern unfurls in an unseen breeze. The port side of the boat, the sunset side, is silver, reflecting the silver sheen of the cove water. The starboard side is white. The boot tops, cove stripe, and gunwale trace the boat's sheer in perfect parallel symmetry. The stanchions and spinnaker pole and bow pulpit are also silver. The forest behind the boat is a deep, dark green, almost black, and only with close examination can you make out gray trunks of individual trees. Everything teeters between darkness and light. But what is most notable is the light: it is a light that vibrates, that shimmers, that almost seems to be alive, as if you can somehow see the individual, shimmering quanta of light. It is a fragile light, light on the cusp of something.

19 What? You need a passport?

My sister reports that when she and her family crossed into Canada the winter after Will's accident the authorities demanded passports, a new policy of which my sister was unaware.

"They wanted Will's passport," she says, "but what I wanted to tell them was why did they need Will's passport when they already had Will's arm?"

20 Turns

We look for turning points because turning points make life more comprehensible. Will's accident marks a turn, at least with regard to Desolation Sound, when beauty and violence twined together, when a great love and a great horror fused into one thing. If a year after Will lost his arm I no longer dreamed my sister's scream, I also no longer considered myself an optimist: my perspective had darkened, perhaps the inevitable result of sixty years on the planet. But it seems to me it was more like one of those post-Renaissance paintings by Rembrandt or Vermeer that seem to become richer but sadder over time.

Still, I had begun to feel as if I couldn't wait to go back to British Columbia. Not to Walsh Cove, perhaps. Not even to the yacht club outstation (I couldn't bear the thought of answering questions about Will with the bravado that such questions seem to demand: that Will was brave, that Will was overcoming his handicap, that the family was hanging in there, even if these statements were all true). We would sail north, I decided, but we would seek new harbors, new coves, new passages that bore no weight from the past. We would not forgo forging new memories even if that were the only way to avoid painful ones and we would not forgo the truth of past memories even if that were the only balm to ease our pain.

So in July 2007 my wife Susan and my son John and I headed north and west, past Desolation Sound, up Johnstone Strait, to the Broughton Islands. Where there'd be fewer boats. Where everything would be new. Where we would hear whales sing, see mountains perpetually capped by snow, walk in forests that come down to the water's edge, watch waterfalls veil granite cliffs, sail on currents that swirled and tumbled through narrow passages, listen to eagles scream and heron croak, watch black bears ramble across rocky beaches, follow misted passages that beckoned us beyond the next turn.

And it works.

There is one moment in particular, a morning in a solitary cove in Hopetown Passage in Mackenzie Sound. Rain has fallen all night, drumming on the cabin top, dappling the water's surface, fogging the windows of the canvas cockpit dodger. My son and my wife are still asleep in their bunks. I rig a hose and shower nozzle to the cockpit freshwater outlet because I plan to shower topside *au natural.* I slip out of my sweatpants and I feel the cool air and the cold rain against my skin and I spray myself with the shower and then I secure the nozzle and I soap myself in the rain and there is in this moment, in this empty cove, among the trees and the mountains and the rain, something cleansing, something magical.

Might the best moments in life get better—dare we hope?—if contrasted against the worst?

21 Reunion

My sister calls me in July 2007, before we leave for Desolation Sound, the year after Will lost his arm. "We may come up," she says, "and we'd like to meet you, but we're not totally certain, because the family and I made a deal: if anybody wants to turn back, we turn back—no questions asked."

22 Three Images

When I think about sailing in British Columbia, I think of three images. The first is from several years ago—I captured it on video. We're in Walsh Cove, my sister's family with us, and it's high tide. My sister and her daughters Elizabeth and Catherine are dancing on a reef. They are high-kicking but the reef is underwater so you can't see that they're standing on it and there is in the video, in its simplicity, in their high kicks, a sense of unadorned and unaffected joy. The second image is a snapshot—for months we kept it on our refrigerator door in Seattle—and it was taken the week after Will lost his arm. It's of my son John and his cousin, Alexandra, and they are each on an air mattress and they are floating in Pendrell Sound, not far from Walsh Cove, and they are head-to-head and they are talking to each other and they are oblivious to the photographer or to anybody else and there is in this moment, it seems to me, the element of family and connecting to family. And the third image—I have no photo of this—is of my nephew, William G.; the time is summer 2007, the year after Will lost his arm, and Will and his family *have* come to Desolation Sound and Will is standing on a cliff above Lake Unwin in Desolation Sound and he is preparing to jump from the cliff, thirty feet above the lake, repeating what he has done so many times before but also what he has never done before because he has never jumped with only one arm and he is holding his good arm up in the air and it is this moment, the instant before he jumps, that I see courage and hope and perseverance, that I see Will G. alive, and, maybe, what I see is Paradise returning.

The Monadnock Essay Collection Prize

This contest was started to encourage essayists to gather their work into book form. The prize is awarded for a book-length collection (120-160 pages or 50,000-60,000 words) of nonfiction essays. The essays can take any form: personal essays, memoir in essay form, narrative nonfiction, commentary, travel, historical account etc.

For more guidelines please go to our web page: www.bauhanpublishing.com/the-monadnock-essay-collection-prize

Neil Mathison is the first winner of this annual contest.